KNOW THE
LAW
HANDBOOK

KNOW THE LAW HANDBOOK

Edited by
PETER ROBERTS

PAUL HAMLYN · LONDON

Published by

PAUL HAMLYN LTD

Westbook House · Fulham Broadway
London

© 1963 Paul Hamlyn Ltd

Printed in Czechoslovakia

T 1224

Contents

		PAGE
Editor's Note	. . . .	6

CHAPTER

1. Problems in Everyday Life	. . . .	9
2. Marriage and Divorce	. . . .	37
3. Children	. . . . . .	67
4. Wills and Testaments	. . . .	91
5. Buying, Business and Bankruptcy	. . . . . .	105
6. Motoring	. . . .	149
7. House Purchase	. . . . .	187
8. Landlord and Tenant	. . . .	221
9. Problems at Work	. . . . .	243
10. The Courts	. . . . . .	257
11. Solicitors and Barristers	. . . .	267
12. Some Legal Terms	. . . .	279
Index	. . . .	301

The law does not restrain our freedom: it maintains it; and, as a great advocate said long ago, where law ends tyranny begins.

Law is reason, and although the reasoning of some laws is shrouded in the mist of antiquity, it is usually good sound reason. English law is not (as Mr Bumble said in *Oliver Twist*) an ass: it is a living, changing thing that provides for us security and the freedom from oppression that we in this country have long taken as our heritage.

In these pages you will find some 300 questions and answers on English law, several examples of contracts of different types, and a glossary of legal terms. But a book of this length cannot pretend to cover each subject completely, and it is intended only as a broad guide on some of the many problems in life today. The law is too complex even for many of the questions here to be fully answered – if some of them were, they would occupy several books of this size.

The law also changes very quickly in our modern fast-moving life. What was good law yesterday may be obsolete today: what

is lawful today may be unlawful tomorrow –
and frequently is. So please do not hold this
book aloft in Court, expecting it to confound
Her Majesty's Judges with its wisdom. Use it
more as a general guide, so that if you have
a problem you can approach a solicitor
with at least some working knowledge of
the subject.

Nobody need lack for legal advice or
the assistance of a solicitor in most types of
court cases, because there is a subsidised
Legal Aid Scheme. There are also Citizens'
Advice Bureaux in most towns where sen-
sible, practical information can be obtained
on many simple legal problems. In some
towns there are also poor man's lawyers.

PROBLEMS IN EVERYDAY LIFE

PROBLEMS IN EVERYDAY LIFE

What is libel?

Every person has the right to protect his good name and his reputation. Just as an injury can be done to the body, a name can be injured by false statements made against a person. Libel is a statement that is published in print – or in writing – that tends to expose a man to hatred, contempt or ridicule. It can take various forms: it may be in the form of printed words in a newspaper, a cartoon, a painting, a photograph, or even a letter written to a friend. An aircraft's skywriting was once held to be libellous, as was a film and its sound track. Libel must reduce a man in other people's estimation; no amount of abuse written about a person is libellous unless it does this.

What is slander?

The spoken defamation of character. Slander differs from libel in that it is not written or drawn for all to see. For a successful action of slander to be brought, one must usually have suffered some definite damage – in business, in social life, etc. There are, however, certain types of slander that permit a court action without proof of any special damages. They are: *(a)* if the slander implies that the person has committed a crime for which he should be imprisoned; *(b)* if it disparages anyone in his trade, profession, etc.; *(c)* if it imputes that the plaintiff was suffering from certain diseases; *(d)* if it imputes unchastity to any woman. Slander can include the spoken word, deaf and dumb language, or inarticulate but significant sounds. An action for slander may be taken if the statement has been made to one person – the number of people who hear a slanderous statement does not matter. And if a person repeats slanderous gossip he can be sued in the same way as if he were the originator of the statement: it is no defence to say, 'I heard the story from so-and-so.'

What is a tort?

This word keeps recurring in any legal dealings one may have about problems in everyday life, and it often leads to confusion in the minds of the public. Lawbreaking is divided into two categories: public wrongs, which are dealt with by the Crown and are punishable; and private wrongs, for which an action for damages or an injunction may be brought against the wrongdoer by a private person. Private wrongs are again divided into the breaking of a contract, and the failure to perform a duty. The last category is called a tort. Committing a nuisance such as making excessive noise, or trespassing, negligence, obstruction and so on, are classed as torts. A tort, or failure of duty, can be committed by not doing something which one should do or by doing something one should not do. However, there are many failures of duty which the Courts do not recognise.

What can be done about a neighbour's noisy radio?

This is one of the great nuisances of our time, especially now that transistor sets are so popular. One can bring a private action for nuisance and apply for an injunction, although this is expensive and sometimes difficult to prove. If three neighbours get together and complain that the radio is seriously disrupting their normal way of life – disturbing their sleep, perhaps – then they can report it as a public nuisance and it will be dealt with by the Police. The noise, whether from a radio, or children, or piano-playing, must be fairly serious in order to be successfully stopped, as the law says that there must be a certain amount of give and take in our crowded island. Most lease agreements for flats contain clauses to restrain the tenants from making too much noise.

Is the making of noise at night considered a nuisance even though it happens only once?

Yes, any excessive noise made at night is illegal. A case involving a woman who owned a silver fox farm, and a local farmer, is one of the most famous on this subject. It appears that at the time when most of the bitches were about to give birth the farmer one night took his shotgun to the boundary of the fox owner's land and discharged it, with disastrous results. He had to pay considerable damages.

If a man sets up a repair garage in a residential area, can he be stopped from making a noise in the normal pursuit of his trade?

Yes, if sufficient people (usually three) complain that the noise seriously disturbs them. Factories housing noisy machinery

Excessive noise at night is illegal

must be built away from houses, unless their owners can prove that a similarly noisy trade has been carried on at the site for twenty years. Even then they can in certain circumstances be restrained. This also applies to trades, such as tanning, which emit an unpleasant smell.

If a person plants a tree (or hedge) which in time grows so large that it excludes light from his next-door neighbour's valuable flower beds, can he be sued?

No. This is reasonable use of his own land and would not be considered a nuisance. But if any branches overhung the neighbour's garden he could tell the owner of the tree to trim them back, or he could trim them himself. The branches and any fruit that may be on them belong to the owner of the tree.

If a person constructs a window in his own house that overlooks his neighbour's garden can he be made to close it up again?

No. This again is reasonable use of his land. But the neighbour can put up a screen if he gets town planning permission, or register a notice under the Rights of Light Act which has the same legal effect.

This new building will obstruct his 'right of light'

Can a builder be prevented from erecting a house so close to another that it lessens the light coming through windows?

If the house is less than nineteen years and one day old it has no 'right of light'. If it (or any previous house on the site with a similar window) has enjoyed uninterrupted light for more than that time, as a general rule a building must not be erected so that it obstructs light coming in at an angle of up to 45 degrees. It seems hard, but if a fairly new house is built so that its windows have a fine view nothing can be done to prevent anyone building a house that obstructs that view, as long as town planning and by-laws are obeyed.

If the roots of a tree penetrate into a neighbour's garden may they be cut off?

Yes, and often are. Roots that grow under another's land may well be under his house as well, causing the land to settle, or the foundations to crack or shift. This case is very simple to prove, just by exposing the roots and getting a competent witness to see them. The roots may be cut without letting the owner know, even if it kills the tree. The law allows this to be done because it is occasionally necessary to remove roots fairly quickly to save a building.

Must a house-owner fence his garden?

The title deeds to the house may require this. Otherwise he is under no obligation to do so, either between his neighbour's garden and his own or where his garden follows the public road. If a person's garden fence falls down and looks unsightly his neighbour has no right to ask him to rebuild it.

How is the responsibility for a garden fence decided?

Where the land is divided into building plots the plans often state on which side of the boundary the garden fence is to be erected. If the plot is an old one and plans are not clear, then as a rough guide the owner is usually the party occupying the land to which the fence posts face. Sometimes, however, a fence is party property and the responsibility is shared.

If a bonfire prevents a neighbour enjoying his garden can it be prevented?

If the bonfire is made regularly and frequently one may take action through

Smoke from a bonfire ruins this siesta

the Court; but if it is merely made every few weeks, of garden rubbish, it would be considered reasonable, no matter how much it may spoil a Sunday afternoon sleep in the garden. Even if the bonfire constitutes a nuisance (in law) it would be unwise to attempt to extinguish it with the garden hose!

If the owner of a piece of land is not known and cannot be found may anyone use it?

This is covered by the Limitations Act, which states that action for the recovery of land may not be made by any private person after twelve years have elapsed. If such a plot of land next to a person's garden has been used for twelve years as his own, without payment of rent or other admission that it belongs to another, he is entitled to keep it. But if he has built on it before that time and the original owner turns up, he will have to give the land and all that is on it back to the owner.

How effective is the notice 'Trespassers will be prosecuted'?

This notice has very little legal power. Certainly an owner may bring an action against a trespasser, but he will almost certainly receive very nominal damages, for the trespasser will usually only have trampled a little grass. An owner of land is entitled to tell a trespasser to get off his land by the shortest route. If his request is refused he may then remove the trespasser by reasonable physical force.

If a tree on someone's land falls and injures a passer-by is the owner liable?

It has been said that 'a tree is not a dangerous animal' and so the owner is not liable for a hidden defect in it. But if the tree is very old and can be seen to be diseased the owner would be at fault for not cutting it down.

Who is responsible for claims if a racing car skids off the track and injures spectators?

If the organisers have taken reasonable care to protect the spectators, by safety fencing, ditches and so on, they are not responsible for damages. People who watch a dangerous sport must accept a certain amount of risk. However, race organisers are usually insured against this type of accident.

If a coal hole in the pavement is left open while the coal is delivered and someone falls down it, can the merchant be sued?

Yes. This amounts to negligence, even though it may happen in broad daylight.

If a visitor has an accident in a person's house is the occupier liable for any damages?

People who enter houses apart from the occupier fall into three categories: a licensee, who may be a friend entering the house as a visitor; an invitee, who may be the window cleaner; trespassers, who are there without authority. A trespasser must take the house as he finds it – the owner is under very little obligation to ensure his safety. But an owner must not set injurious traps, even for a trespasser – mantraps were made illegal many years ago. An owner must not act recklessly against a trespasser: a case was once heard involving an innocent trespasser who decided to snooze under a tree. The owner felled the tree and subsequently it was held that he should have known the trespasser was under it; damages were awarded to the trespasser. The owner's duty towards a guest is that he must warn him of any concealed danger that he knows about – rotten floorboards, bad electrical connections, etc. An invitee – who could be a customer in a shop, or a plumber in a private house – must be warned about any concealed danger of which the owner knows *or ought to know*. If an owner fails to warn about any of these points he is liable for damages that may be claimed in case of an accident. Many comprehensive household insurance policies cover these risks under 'householder's liability'.

If an uninsured errand boy on a bicycle seriously injures a pedestrian, can damages be claimed?

They may be claimed, but the injured party would find some difficulty in enforcing payment. After a successful action, an order may possibly be made for 5s a week, but even if paid for the remainder of the boy's life it may not cover a fraction of the damages. If a pedestrian is permanently injured his only recourse is to his National Insurance schemes or National Assistance. Many people consider that cycle insurance should be compulsory like motor insurance. Incidentally, the insurance companies have set up a fund for the compensation of people injured by uninsured cars, and make *ex gratia* payments from it when a case arises.

If a person accidentally injures another with his umbrella in the street is he liable?

Yes, if negligence can be proved – and this type of accident is usually caused by negligence, however small. Most insurance companies have a 'personal liability' policy which will cover a whole family for this kind of mishap. The charge is small – about 10s – and the cover is often for as much as £10,000.

If a pedestrian falls into a depression in the road, is the local council liable?

If the depression (pot-holes, etc.) has appeared through the normal wear and tear of the highway the local council would not be liable; but if it were caused by bad workmanship on the part of the council employees, then they could be sued for damages. If it were ringed with red warning lights or barriers they would not be liable.

The local authorities have the same responsibilities whether an accident occurs in daylight or darkness. In most small cases, such as when someone has tripped over a paving stone which is not level with the others, a plaintiff would find the case very difficult to prove, as it can so easily be argued that the other paving stones had settled and that the one the pedestrian tripped over was the only one of the correct level!

If a cow strays from a field and a motorist hits it can the owner of the cow be sued?

A farmer is under no obligation to fence in his animals from the adjoining highway, and the law says that motorists must put up with the cattle and the farmer must put up with the motorists.

How much does a dog licence cost?

It costs 7s 6d, is obtainable at a post office, and must be renewed every year. A licence is not needed for a puppy of under six months, for guide dogs used by the blind, or for sheep dogs. The fine for keeping an unlicensed dog is £5. A dog is the only animal that must be licensed in Britain, although a farmer must have permission to keep a bull in his field.

If a dog runs into a neighbour's garden and ruins a vegetable patch can the neighbour sue the owner for damages?

Cats and dogs cannot be guilty of trespass, as it is said to be 'in their nature' to wander and scratch the earth.

If cattle get into a private garden and destroy it can the owner of the cattle be sued?

Yes. Under an old law the owner of the garden can, if he wishes, impound the cattle until recompense has been made. The cost of housing and feeding the animals would be added to the damages. Or he can sue for trespass.

What is the effect of putting a 'Beware of the Dog' notice on a gaet?

Very little, if the dog bites a postman. The law actually allows a dog his first bite, as it considers that the owner cannot know about his dog's bad ways until it has shown any. The second bite is a different matter: then an order for keeping the dog under control may be made by the Court. On a third occasion the order will usually be one that demands that the dog is destroyed. If it is not complied with, the owner is faced with a fine of £1 a day. An appeal to a higher Court may be made against the destruction of the dog, but the owner will need to have some very good reasons. Damages can be claimed only when it can be proved that the dog owner knew of his pet's bad habits.

May a person shoot a dog he finds ruining his garden?

No, unless the dog is dangerous to human or other animal life at the time.

If a dog savages a trespasser, has he any redress?

If dogs are deliberately set on a person walking through a farmer's land the trespasser may certainly claim damages, but if watchdogs are left all night in a garden and a trespasser is mauled by them there is no liability.

Is the owner responsible for this?

If a pet rabbit disappears and later is found to be living in a neighbour's garden, can its original owner demand it back?

A rabbit is classed as a wild animal and cannot be owned completely. Anyone who takes and tames it is the owner, until the animal decides to leave him. Then the owner is the next person who takes and tames it. Wild animals can only be owned completely when they are dead. An example has been given in court of a swarm of bees belonging to a person and hived in his garden. When the bees decided to change their address the first owner could not claim them back again.

May one walk out of a restaurant if a meal is below standard?

If he finds a meal uneatable a client may try it, if he has the courage! But he would be wiser to give his name and address to the manager, and tell him that the meal was below standard and that he refused to pay. The management could then sue (for the cost of the meal only) if they were willing to take the risk, and face the likely publicity.

If a restaurant meal makes a client ill, can he sue?

Only if he can prove that the meal did in fact make him ill. He must prove negligence against the proprietor. To prove negligence one must establish two things: *(a)* that the defendant owed a duty towards him, and *(b)* that he failed to do that duty, and in failing caused the damage.

Does the notice in a hotel stating that the management is not responsible for loss of goods in the hotel actually relieve them of responsibility?

It relieves them of a certain amount, but not all. The management will generally only have to recompense a guest for loss up to £30 from rooms, unless his staff were negligent. A hotelier exhibits the notice to reduce his liability, not to be free of it. He cannot be held liable for theft by a burglar who may break into a room.

May a hotel proprietor keep a guest's luggage if he cannot pay the bill?

Yes, and he sometimes finds that this is the only way to recover his money. He is

31

said to have a *lien* on the goods, and may keep them until he receives payment. No hotel keeper can detain a guest for not paying his bill, so the fear of being consigned to the kitchens as washer-up need not disturb you.

If a person books a hotel room and then fails to arrive, can the hotelier claim the full charges?

He is entitled to recover his loss. If he had not been able to rent the room for the period booked he may claim for the full amount. If, however, the rooms had been cancelled in good time there is no claim. If a deposit has been placed and the rooms cancelled in good time and relet, the deposit should be returned.

If a travel agent describes a foreign hotel as much better than it is in fact, may his customer, who is compelled to stay there, sue him?

Yes – this would be a breach of contract, and the agent may be sued for damages. Support to such a case could be given by other people who may be staying in the same hotel – and who would probably be in the same predicament.

If a person commits a civil wrong and dies before an action can be brought to court, does the case die with him?

An action in tort dies with the defendant. If the action was for a breach of contract, however, it would pass to his estate through his executors. For example, a person who had signed a contract for the building of a house died before the work could be started. His estate (money, etc., left in his will) was debited with several hundred pounds, the loss of profit that the builder would have made if he had carried the job through.

Is 'findings keepings'?

No. If an article has been found in a public place the fact must be reported to the Police. If the finder keeps it without reporting, he may be guilty of 'stealing by finding'. However, he may after a time (one month for ordinary property, or six months for valuables) claim the article if the rightful owner has not already done so.

How may a person change his name?

Simply by using another name. If John Smith wants to call himself John Brown, he may do so just by changing his signature and telling friends and business associates. No other formality is necessary, although if a person wishes he may change his name by deed poll, which is merely used as an official way of recording and advertising the new name. In fact, most people use this latter method today. There are some dangers in changing a name. If a small motor manufacturer were to change his name to Mr. Bentley, and commence to use his name on his product, he might expect a vigorous protest from another company!

Do solicitors base their fees on any general scale?

The Law Society lays down scales of charges for property transactions; there are also scales of County Court costs. For other services a solicitor charges according to the complexity of the matter, the difficulty or novelty of questions raised, the skill involved in the work, the number of documents prepared, and the importance of the matter to the client. It is often very difficult for a solicitor to assess the costs of his services at the beginning of his work – he can only tell the client that he will advise him when the costs rise above a certain sum. Any client may query a solicitor's bill by telling him that he would like the Law Society to approve it before payment is made.

Must the railway authority always pay compensation to passengers hurt in a crash?

Normally they are insured to cover such contingencies, but in any case if the accident arises from negligence they would be responsible in law – and most rail crashes are attributable to some human failing. But if the accident is proved unavoidable, then the railway authority is not liable. A jury once put it like this: 'The obligation of the company in such a case to take good care included the duty of exercising all vigilance to provide whatever was required for the safe conveyance of their passengers, but it did not subject the company to the plain injustice of being compelled by law to make reparation for a disaster due to a latent defect in machinery which no human skill could have detected.'

If a late train causes a commercial traveller to lose a big order can the railway authorities be sued?

The British Railways invite a person to travel on their trains, but do not guarantee the time of arrival, even though it may be published in a time-table. The published time of arrival merely shows intent. The ticket itself is the contract that the railways make with the traveller, and no mention is made of time on it.

MARRIAGE AND DIVORCE

What are the minimum requirements for a legal marriage?

A licence to marry, the taking of the marriage vows before a registrar, and the signing of the marriage certificate. The minimum age for marriage (with parents' consent) is 16. The minimum age without consent is 21, except under Scottish Law where, providing the residential qualifications are in order, a couple may be married without parents' consent under the age of 21.

Must both parents consent to the marriage of their child who is under twenty-one?

If both parents are living together the consent of both is necessary; if they are living apart (divorced, separated, etc.), the consent of the parent who has legal custody of the child is necessary; if one of the parents has been deserted by the other, only the consent of the deserted parent is necessary. When the Court considers that consent is unreasonably withheld, it may give permission for the marriage. Legal marriages no longer take place over the anvil at Gretna Green, but young people still go there in order to live in Scotland and qualify as residents.

Set out below is a copy of a Marriage Certificate,

CERTIFIED COPY OF AN ENTRY OF MARRIAGE

REGISTRATION DISTRICT: *Harlow*

1962 Marriage solemnized at: *The Parish Church* in the

Columns	1	2	3	4
No.	When married	Name and Surname	Age	Condition
132	June 29th 1962	Arthur John Porter	28	Bachelor
		Joan Ann Bishop	23	Spinster

Married in the *Parish Church* according to the Rites of the:

This marriage was solemnized by us	}	*Arthur John Porter*	in the presence of us	}
		Joan Ann Bishop		

---

showing the various entries that must be made

PURSUANT TO THE MARRIAGE ACTS 1949 and 1954

Parish of *Winterden* **in the County of** *Surrey*

5	6	7	8
Rank or Profession	**Residence at time of marriage**	**Father's name and surname**	**Rank or Profession**
Clerk	*Wayside The Common Winterden*	*George John Porter*	*Deceased*
Secretary	*61 Princes Road Dorking*	*Edward William Bishop*	*Farmer*

Church of England

Jeremy John Porter   *J. G. Whitfield (Vicar)*

Maude Rose Bishop

At what time of day may a marriage take place?

Usually between the hours of 8 a.m. and 6 p.m. unless a special licence allows the marriage to take place at any time convenient to the couple. It is not advisable to ask a minister of the Church to marry you on a Sunday!

How does one arrange to be married at a church?

A convenient date must be fixed with the minister, and the banns are published for three Sundays preceding the ceremony. This simply means that the details of the forthcoming marriage are read out in a church. One of the parties must have lived in the parish in which the marriage is to take place for at least twenty-one days. Banns must be published in the parish church of each of the two parties, if they live in different parishes. A registrar will be in attendance at the church and the couple must sign their marriage certificate after the church ceremony.

What is a registry office marriage?

A civil marriage held in the registry

After the marriage ceremony

office (where the simple vows required by law are taken) without a ceremony at a church. Two witnesses are needed, and the ceremony must take place 'with open doors' – i.e. it must not be in private.

What is a special licence, and how is it obtained?

There are various forms of special licence, most of which reduce the necessary waiting period. This period may be reduced to as little as two days, depending on circumstances, such as if one of the parties is shortly leaving the country for service abroad, or a similar emergency. One usually has to apply to an Archbishop for a special licence.

What are the kinship restrictions to marriage?

The laws of Church and State say that a man may not marry his:

Mother	Wife's daughter
Daughter	Father's wife
Father's mother	Son's wife
Mother's mother	Father's father's wife

Son's daughter
Daughter's daughter
Sister
Wife's mother
Wife's daughter's
  daughter
Son's son's wife
Daughter's son's
  wife
Father's sister

Mother's father's wife
Wife's father's
  mother
Wife's mother's
  mother
Wife's son's daughter
Mother's sister
Brother's daughter
Sister's daughter

A woman may not marry her:

Father
Son
Father's father
Mother's father
Son's son
Daughter's son
Brother
Husband's father
Husband's son
Daughter's husband
Mother's husband

Husband's father's
  father
Husband's mother's
  father
Husband's son's son
Husband's daughter's son
Son's daughter's
  husband
Daughter's daughter's husband

Father's mother's husband	Father's brother
Mother's mother's husband	Mother's brother
	Sister's son
	Brother's son

Any marriage ceremony between two people of these relationships would be void: i.e. not a legal marriage.

If two people under the age of twenty-one marry in England by falsifying their ages is the marriage legal?

No, the marriage would be void, and the couple could be brought before a Court and fined or imprisoned for committing perjury. If two people married in these circumstances before May 1929, their marriage is valid, as a different law existed in those days.

Are there any other reasons for a marriage to be declared void?

A marriage is void when one party is already married, or of unsound mind, or if one of the parties was married against his or her will – a 'shotgun' wedding would not be a legal ceremony, for example.

If a British subject marries a foreigner abroad, is the marriage valid in Britain?

Yes, if it has been conducted according to the laws of the country in which it took place. However, if a British subject marries a foreigner in England, the marriage may not be valid in the other country if all their laws of marriage have not been observed.

Does an accidental mistake in the marriage certificate make the marriage void?

No, it does not: if one of the parties signs the wrong name, or in the wrong place, or even deliberately gives a wrong age (as long as he or she is over 21) it makes no difference at all.

Is bigamy always a crime?

To be a felony, bigamy (the marriage of a person whose husband or wife is still living and is neither divorced nor has the marriage been declared void) must be

47

deliberate. If, for instance, a wife left her husband over seven years previously and has not been heard of since by her husband and he has made full inquiries in vain, he may reasonably assume that she is dead. If after his second marriage she is found to be alive the second marriage is void, but no proceedings for bigamy would be taken.

Can only a woman sue for breach of promise?

Either a man or a woman can sue, although it is extremely unusual for a man to do so. The law states that if two people have mutually agreed to marry, and one breaks the engagement, the other may sue for damages. However, if they are under 21 they would not have made a binding contract with one another and could not sue. If a man of over 21 is engaged to a girl of less than 21, she may break the engagement without being liable to an action. But if he breaks with her she may sue. In this case the man would have made a legal contract, but the girl, being a minor, could not have done so. Incidentally, if a man breaks the engagement, he is not entitled to take back the girl's ring.

What are the responsibilities of marriage?

Husband and wife have a duty to cohabit (to live together). The husband has a duty to maintain his wife according to his means, and to maintain his wife's children. A wife is never bound to maintain her husband. The husband has the sole right to say where the family home shall be, and the wife has a duty to live there – as long as her husband's decision is reasonable.

Is a husband responsible for debts that his wife incurred before they were married?

No. Any debts, contracts, pending court actions, etc., that a wife was involved in before her marriage are her affair, although a husband usually accepts as much responsibility as he can.

Is a husband responsible for any tort (civil wrong) that his wife may commit?

No, a husband cannot be sued or held responsible for his wife's acts unless he authorised them.

Are the savings a wife may take out of house-keeping her own?

No, they belong to her husband, and if she wins any prize with them the prize also belongs to her husband; but the tendency of the Courts is now to improve the wife's position in family financial matters.

Is a husband responsible for a debt his wife may incur during marriage – a large grocer's bill, for example?

Yes, if she incurred them as his 'agent'. He must maintain his family, and so he must pay for the necessities of life. But if he finds that she is very extravagant, he may tell her not to buy certain items; if she continues to do so he would have the right not to assume responsibility, even though the tradesmen did not know of his instructions at the time. A curious case occurred when a wife began divorce proceedings against her husband, and later abandoned them. It was ruled that the cost was one of the necessities of life, and that the husband was responsible for them!

Is the taking of a husband's name by a wife optional?

Yes, it is. There are many prominent

The husband is presented with his wife's debts

people who do not use their husband's name. Dr Edith Summerskill (now Baroness Summerskill) is an example of a woman who continues to use her own name after marriage. (Her husband's name is Dr Samuels.) Actresses almost always continue to use their own, or their stage names, after their marriage.

If a wife buys an item out of money given to her, does it belong completely to her?

Yes; the law states that anything a wife acquires with her own money is her own property, whether obtained before or after her marriage.

If a wife makes an H. P. contract to buy a washing machine, is the husband responsible for the payments?

Yes; it would usually be understood that she was acting as his agent, even though he did not actually tell her to buy it.

Is a husband responsible for damage done by his wife when trespassing?

He would have been responsible before 1935, but the law was changed at that date and he is no longer liable just because of the fact that he is her husband.

If a husband and wife buy a house, each contributing half the purchase money, to whom does the house belong?

It depends in whose name the house was bought, but if they wish they could sign as joint owners, and each would be entitled to the house in proportion to their contribution. A wife is fully entitled to acquire and hold property and to dispose of it as she wishes – in her will or before her death. It is a long time since the property of the wife became the property of the husband on marriage!

To whom does the 'Family Allowance' belong?

It belongs to the wife, unless her husband can show that it is unwise to let her have it.

Should a husband make a new will after marriage?

Yes; marriage revokes any previous will made by the husband (*see* Wills).

53

May a married woman act as executrix (a person who helps to see that the wishes of the testator are carried out) of a will?

Yes. A married woman may administer a will, just as if she were single, but any contracts she makes – or any trouble she may get into – is not the responsibility of her husband.

Can a wife be compelled to give evidence against her husband?

In criminal cases a wife cannot be called to give evidence unless he, as the prisoner, wishes. If he is charged with an offence against his wife, then she may be called without his approval.

Who is responsible for tradesmen's debts when an unmarried couple are living together as man and wife?

The man has the same obligations as if they were married, and the tradesmen are entitled to the same treatment. An unmarried couple having set up as man and wife, the man must assume many of the legal responsibilities of a husband.

What are the grounds for divorce?

A wife or husband may petition for a divorce on the following grounds:

1. That the other has committed adultery since the marriage.

2. That one party has deserted the other without good cause for a period of three years immediately preceding the presentation of the petition.

3. That one party has treated the other with cruelty since the marriage.

4. That one party is incurably of unsound mind and has been continuously under care and treatment for a period of at least five years immediately preceding the presentation of the petition.

5. That the husband (only) has, since the marriage, been guilty of rape or an unnatural offence.

How is adultery proved?

Naturally, adultery is difficult to prove outright, but it is usually considered to be proved if one of the parties is found in circumstances in which adultery was extremely likely to have taken place – i. e. spending a night in a hotel room with a member of the opposite sex.

What is the legal definition of desertion?

Simple desertion means that one party has left the other without good reason and against the other's will. But a wife need not have left her husband's house for him to petition on the grounds of desertion: if she refuses to cook his meals, keep house, live with him as man and wife, these neglects *might* also add up to desertion in the eyes of the law. If the husband's conduct at home is deliberately calculated to drive his wife out of the house – and he succeeds – then he would have deserted her by 'constructive desertion'. To be called desertion, the move must be without cause, and ordinary disagreements and quarrels are not usually considered sufficient cause. If a husband and wife agree to live apart, there is no desertion.

What is meant by cruelty?

Cruelty falls into two categories. Physical cruelty, which means violence or ill-treatment, and 'mental cruelty' – although this is not a legal term in England – which means continual behaviour on the part of one partner which is intended to make life together impossible and which is likely over the years to injure the health of the other. Again, ordinary arguments and domestic quarrels are not usually considered sufficient cause to petition on the grounds of cruelty.

Does English Law recognise foreign divorce decrees?

Yes, if the decree is recognised by the Courts of the domicile (the country in which they have their permanent home) of the parties.

For what reasons would a petition for divorce fail?

The bars to a petition are: *Connivance*, when it can be proved that the complaining partner knew of the adultery or other offence at the time it happened and either approved or encouraged it, or ignored it, or made no move to prevent it happening. *Collusion*, when the husband and wife make a bargain under which one of them will divorce the other. *Condonation*, in which, say, a husband forgives an offence by his wife: if an offence is forgiven it is blotted out legally, and cannot later be used as grounds for a divorce suit. If, however, the wife later deserts her husband he may use the offence as grounds, even though the desertion is for a comparatively short time. *Adultery* by the petitioner (the party seeking the divorce) is often a bar to the divorce, although in some cases the Court uses its 'discretion'. For instance, if a wife has been driven by cruelty from her home and eventually sets up house with a man who can provide her with food and shelter, the Court may favour her petition for divorce, recognising that she could do little else. Similarly if a wife deserts her husband, leaving him and their children without a woman to look after them, he may ask another woman to live in his house; the law might also look on this type of case favourably. *Conducing*, which is the encouragement or exposure of the other partner to adultery, by perhaps using her as bait to draw players into a gaming house. If a wife is then free with her favours, it is considered the husband's fault. *Delay* in presenting a petition for divorce is also looked on with suspicion by the Court, and a good explanation must be given or the petition may be dismissed.

How does one begin proceedings for divorce?

Before beginning any action it is advisable to have the guidance and the services of a solicitor. Basically, a petition for divorce is presented, filed and eventually heard by the Court. A petition is 'sworn on oath' – it is an appeal to the Court that the marriage be dissolved for such and such a reason, that (in the case of a wife's petition) adequate maintenance is provided, and that the custody of the children is settled, and so on. The petition is served on the husband (or wife) who may then file a defence, or decide not to defend the suit. The Court that deals with divorce is the Probate, Divorce and Admiralty Division of the High Court of Justice in London, or an Assize Court in provincial regions. Unfortunately there are often such long waiting lists that a petitioner may have to wait anything between six and nine months for hearing.

Is there any difference in procedure if the other partner decides to defend the suit?

If a suit is undefended by the other party, then the petitioner merely gives evidence as to why the divorce should be granted. If the evidence is sufficient the divorce is granted, but the other party must have had warning of the case. If the suit is defended, the other partner will have a barrister present to cross-examine. The defence may be merely for the purpose of preventing the divorce, or it may be a counter-petition. The result in this case may be that the judge will grant the original divorce, or support the defendant's counter, petition, or refuse a divorce on either side, or even on rare occasions grant both partners a divorce.

After the case has been heard and a divorce granted is the decision final?

No; normally the Court will grant a decree *nisi* (which means 'unless'), and for a further three months the marriage is still in force. Then after three months have elapsed a decree *absolute* is given (unless further evidence that would bar the divorce is uncovered) and the marriage is finally broken. There is no appeal after a divorce has been made absolute.

What is a separation order?

A wife deserted by her husband may apply to the Court for a separation order which makes provision for her and her children. An order can also be made on the application of the wife if her husband has been convicted of an assault on her, if he has been persistently cruel to her, or if he has been guilty of wilful neglect of her or their children. If the wife returns to her husband and lives with him after an order has been obtained, even for a brief time, the order is cancelled.

Judicial separation can, in fact, be obtained for the same reasons as the grounds for divorce – it is really a lesser form of divorce, one which need not be permanent and requires no remarriage if the parties wish to live together again.

What is a maintenance order?

If a husband wrongfully refuses to maintain his wife and the children, she can apply to a Magistrates' Court for a maintenance order, which will demand that her husband pay her up to £7 15s od a week for herself and £2 10s od a week for each child. If her husband's income is high, he may be required to pay considerably more by a higher Court.

When can a wife apply for a maintenance order?

She may apply before she has left her husband (for cruelty, adultery, etc.) as the Court realises that she may not have enough money of her own to start a new home. But she must leave her husband within three months of the granting of a maintenance order.

If a husband stops paying maintenance after a few months, what action can a wife take?

She can let the Court know that its order has been ignored. If this state of affairs lasts for some time the husband (or ex-husband if they have been divorced) could be sent to prison.

What is a co-respondent?

If a wife has committed adultery the person with whom she misbehaved is the co-respondent. Usually he cannot be sued for damages – although this depends on the amount of influence he had on the wife – but he may have to pay the husband's costs in a successful divorce case. If the husband is the defendant, his wife can later sue the 'other woman' for *loss of consortium*.

What is the usual cost of divorce?

This depends on the complexity of the case, the number of witnesses, and so on. If it is a simple undefended case it might cost about £80. Legal aid may be sought if the petitioner thinks he cannot afford to pay the cost. The system of legal aid bases the proportion the petitioner has to pay on the amount he is able to afford, which is assessed by the National Assistance Board. If the entire fees and charges are paid under the system, the petitioner cannot choose his own lawyer. Application should be made for legal aid before any proceedings begin.

What proportion of his income must a husband pay to a wife who has divorced him?

Although it is not a strict rule, the Court usually orders that the wife should have one-third of their joint incomes. For example if she earns £200 a year and the husband £700, he would be ordered to pay her £100 a year, and if she earned nothing he would have to part with £233 13s 4d a year. An order may at times be made in favour of the wife even when her husband has divorced her.

When husbands or wives put a case to the Court is it heard in public?

If a wife wishes the Court to issue an order against her husband – separation, maintenance, etc., – she may apply to a Magistrates' Court. There the Court is made up of three magistrates, one of whom is usually a woman. During the hearing the public is not allowed into the Court and the press are allowed to report only the broad outlines of the case. This is to shield people from undue publicity and to help to mend the marriage, if possible.

These matrimonial hearings come under 'Domestic Proceedings'.

May the Church refuse to marry a divorced person?

Yes, a clergyman is under no obligation to marry a couple, one of whom is divorced and whose ex-partner is still living.

To whom does the house and furniture belong after a divorce?

The items a husband bought out of his own money belong to him. These usually amount to house, furniture, ornaments, cars, washing machines – more or less everything in a normal household where the wife has not been in outside employment. Anything he has given her – jewellery, clothes and so on, are, of course, her own. Half the money in a joint bank account also belongs to the wife, no matter how little she has herself put into the account.

If a wife who has divorced her husband remarries does she lose her maintenance?

Usually she does, but if an order has been made that she be paid maintenance for her lifetime, she does not.

How is the guardianship of the children decided after divorce?

Unless the two parties have come to an agreement, the Court will decide which is the fitter person to look after them. Every effort will be made to allow the mother to have the young children if this is possible.

CHAPTER THREE

CHILDREN

When is a child illegitimate?

An illegitimate child is one born to parents who are not married to each other. A child born to two unmarried people is illegitimate, and so is a child of one married and one unmarried parent. For example, if a married woman has a child by a man who is not her husband, the child is illegitimate.

If a child is born to an unmarried couple who later marry their child becomes legitimate from the date of their marriage. But if one parent was not in a position to marry at the time of the birth, the child can never be made legitimate, even if the parents married later.

A child is legitimate even if born a day after the marriage of its parents.

Can an illegitimate child inherit if a parent dies without making a will?

If the mother dies intestate, the child has as much right to inherit property and money in the same proportion as any legitimate child. But in the eyes of the law he has no father, so he has no right to the possessions of the person who is in fact his

A birth certificate is often needed later in life, and for this purpose a certified copy, which is laid out as follows, may be drawn up on request.

There is a simpler form of official birth certificate which excludes the father's name and consequently does not reveal whether the person is an illegitimate or adopted child.

CERTIFIED COPY OF AN ENTRY OF BIRTH

PURSUANT TO THE BIRTHS AND DEATHS

Registration District: *Leicester*

1925 birth in the sub-district of *Leicester* **in the County**

No.	Where and when born	Name if any	Sex	Name and surname of father	Name and maiden name of mother
213	*Seventh May 1925 43 London Road Leicester*	*John Peter*	*Boy*	*Frederick William Barnes*	*Jane Barnes formerly Evans*

REGISTRATION ACTS 1836 TO 1929

of *Leicestershire*

Rank or profession of father	Signature description and residence of informant	When registered	Signature of Registrar	Baptismal name if added after registration of birth
Architect	F. W. Barnes Father 43 London Road Leicester	Eighteenth May 1925	J. Rees	

father. If the father wishes to make a will which includes his illegitimate child he must mention the child in his will.

How is a child's birth registered?

The father or mother must inform the Registrar of Births and Deaths of the birth within 42 days of the event. Notification of birth must also be given to the local medical officer of health within 36 hours of the birth. This may be given in writing by the doctor, midwife, father or anyone present at the event.

What is a maternity grant?

It is a sum (£16) which is intended to help with the general expenses of having a baby. It may be paid before or after the birth of the child. It is payable for every child, not only the first.

How is it claimed?

It can be claimed on a husband's or wife's national insurance, providing that it has been properly paid for 26 weeks before the expected birth.

What is a home confinement grant?

It is a sum of £6 which is intended to help with the expense of a birth that does not take place in a public hospital. It is payable whether it takes place at home or in the home of a friend or relative.

What is a maternity allowance?

Expectant mothers who are in employment may claim this allowance so that they may give up work in good time. It is 67s 6d a week payable for 18 weeks, and beginning 11 weeks before the expected birth.

Here is a table setting out the various allowances, who may claim them and how they may be claimed.

What is an infant?

A person under the age of 21. An infant achieves his majority on the first minute of the day *before* his twenty-first birthday. Infants' ages are divided into several smaller categories. The Children and Young Persons Act of 1933 which deals

	BENEFIT	WHO CAN CLAIM
The National Insurance Scheme provides three maternity benefits. Where the conditions for each benefit are satisfied, all three may be paid. They can be paid to both married and single women.	Maternity Grant £14 Additional grants may be paid if more than one baby is born	All Mothers To help with the general expense of having your baby
	Home Confinement Grant £6	All Mothers To help meet the extra expense when your baby is born at home or when you pay the full cost of your maintenance where your baby is born somewhere else (and in certain other exceptional circumstances)
	Maternity Allowance The standard rate is 57s 6d a week normally paid for 18 weeks beginning 11 before the expected week of confinement but not for any time when paid work is done. (The allowance is paid at a reduced rate if the contribution conditions are only partly satisfied)	Mothers doing paid work and paying full insurance contributions. To make it easier for you in the interests of yourself and your baby, to give up work in good time before the birth * You can get this National Insurance Child Welfare (Reproduced by

74

ON WHOSE INSURANCE	HOW TO CLAIM	WHEN TO CLAIM
Either your own or your husband's insurance	With the form you should enclose a form Mat. B. 1 (certificate of expected confinement) form Mat. B.2 — which you can get from your doctor or midwife	Between nine weeks before you expect your baby and three months after it is born.
There are no separate contributions but the conditions for maternity grant must be satisfied	On the form which will have been specially sent to you or else on form B.M.4*	As soon as possible following the birth of your baby, and in any event not later than three months afterwards
Paid only on your own insurance and only when you have recently been paying full Class 1 or Class 2 contributions.	As for Maternity Grant, you should answer all the questions in the section of the form B.M.4* headed "To be completed only if you are claiming Maternity Allowance"	Between the 14th and 11th weeks before you expect your baby, even though you go on working after the 14th week

form from your local Pensions and Office or from the Maternity or Centre

IF YOU DO NOT CLAIM AT THE RIGHT TIME YOU MAY LOSE BENEFIT

permission of the Controller of H. M. Stationery Office)

with the various laws which have been framed basically to protect children, defines a 'child' as an infant up to the age of 14, and a 'young person' as between the ages of 14 and 18. No child under the age of 10 years can be guilty of any offence in law. An infant over 18 and under 21 is as far as criminal law is concerned, an adult, and is liable to the same penalties.

If a young man of twenty is injured by the negligence of a neighbour, can he sue him?

No, he must sue through his parent or guardian, who would be known in Court as his 'next friend'. If he has no parents or guardian he can appoint anyone over 21 to sue for him.

Can a person under twenty-one own property?

No, he cannot hold 'legal interest' in land, buildings, etc., which would be held in trust for him. Any damages that may be awarded to him in an action would also be held in trust by parents or someone appointed by the Court.

Has an unborn child any rights?

For the purpose of inheriting money or property in a will a child *en ventre sa mere* (conceived but not yet born) is considered by law to be born. A bequest can be made to an unborn child in a will.

If a minor buys a motor cycle on hire purchase, and later finds he cannot keep up the payments, can his father be made responsible for them?

No, a father is responsible only for the payment of his child's 'necessaries' such as food, clothing and items needed for education. Generally a child cannot make a legal contract, and is not responsible for his action if he does make a form of contract. However, the party with whom he may have made a form of contract is bound by it if he is over 21 years of age. If a minor defaults on a hire purchase agreement the seller can do very little about it, except to tell the Police, who may institute criminal proceedings for false pretences if the minor has lied about his age.

If a child damages another person's property is his parent liable for damages?

No, a parent cannot be made responsible for his child's torts or civil wrongs. If a child accidentally breaks a window whilst playing cricket in the street his father cannot be made to pay for it. This does not mean that infants are not responsible for their own torts. If it can be proved that there was wrongful intention on the part of the child, he can be held responsible. A father may be liable for damages for his son's tort if he was negligent in permitting the child to commit a tort, i. e. giving a young boy a dangerous gun.

At what age can a child be held responsible for a crime?

Children under the age of 10 are not held responsible for any of their actions and cannot be tried for any crime. Between 10 and 18 they may be brought before a Juvenile Court. They may be punished with a fine on the parents, but it must not be over £2 in the case of a child under

The boy's father cannot be made to pay

14. A child may be sent to an approved school (if he is over 10) or committed to the care of a person of the Court's choosing. Minors of between 12 and 21 may be required to attend attendance centres. Between 14 and 21 they may be sent to a detention centre, and between 16 and 21 they may be sent to a Borstal Institution.

No person under the age of 18 may be sentenced to death, but he may be detained 'at Her Majesty's pleasure'.

What is probation?

When a child commits an offence and the Juvenile Court awards some form of punishment (they never use the word 'sentence') it may be suspended and a probation order made instead. The magistrate tells the offender that he will be put under the care of the probation officer and that if he does not behave himself for the period of probation he may be punished for the offence for which he is in Court. A probation officer is not a police official and has the role of friend and adviser to the offender, who must report to him at regular intervals. Probation officers often arrange accommodation for young people and may also find them work if they have none. Probation is not reserved exclusively for children or young persons, but it is usually ordered for first offenders of any age. Here, too, the philosophy is one of assistance rather than punishment.

At what age may children be employed?

The 1933 Act is very clear about this. One cannot employ a child under 12 years old, it says. That was when the school-leaving age was 14; now that it is 15, one may not employ a child under 13 – i.e. two years under minimum school-leaving age. School children over this age may not be employed *(a)* before the close of school on weekdays, *(b)* between the hours of 8 p. m. and 6 a. m., *(c)* for more than two hours on any school day, *(d)* for more than two hours on a Sunday, *(e)* to lift or carry anything so heavy that it may injure them. No young person under the age of 16 be may employed as a street trader, and most councils have by-laws forbidding it until a person is 18 years old.

May a twelve-year-old singer appear on the stage and earn a fee?

Only just – if he had been a year younger the law would not allow it. A child may not be employed to take part in any entertainment except charity shows – and there are restrictions on these – under the age of 12. If he is over 12 and under 14 he will have to obtain a licence to perform. This may be granted by the local authorities. Nobody may take a young person of under 18 abroad to perform on the stage unless he is over 14 and has been granted a licence.

Is it against the law for a child to buy his father cigarettes?

Yes it is, if the child is under 16. It is also illegal to sell him cigarette papers! If a Court considers that a particular automatic cigarette machine is being used too frequently by children it may order its removal.

How does one adopt a child?

A couple wishing to adopt a child should arrange with one of the various

If she is over twelve she will need a licence

Adoption Societies (the offices of the National Adoption Society are at 47a Manchester Street, London, W.1.) to visit their office. If the society is satisfied that the husband and wife are fit people to adopt a child, they will allow them to choose a child from one of their homes. They will then contact the Children's Officer of the area in which the couple live and arrange for the child to live with them for a probationary period of three months. During this period they will be visited frequently by the authorities, and if they are satisfied at the end of the period an application will be made to the Court for an adoption order. The order is usually made immediately after the probationary period, but during this period the child's mother may claim the return of the child. After the adoption order is signed and the mother's final consent given, the child's birth certificate is destroyed, an adoption certificate made out, and he becomes a full and legal member of his adopted parent's family, enjoying all the rights he would if he were their actual child.

Prospective parents visit an adoption society

Who can adopt a child?

A married couple over 21, a relative over 21, and on rare occasions a single person over 21. The parents of the child may, in certain circumstances, wish to adopt their own child. They may do so at any age. The Court would be reluctant to grant an adoption order to a couple of over 45 years of age, as it is considered that adopting parents should be of less than retiring age when the adopted child would become 21. An application by a male for the adoption of a female child is not usually granted. There is no means test in connection with adoption, but the prospective parents must be able to satisfy the Court that they have a good home.

What are the legal duties of a parent to a child?

The parents have a duty to support and maintain their children until they reach the age of 16, and if they neglect this duty they may be prosecuted. They must also ensure that a child is not exposed to circumstances that may cause it any unnecessary suffering or injury to health. When a child is between the ages of 5 and 15 the parents must comply with the Education Act. – i.e. send him to school. Failure to do so can be punished by fine or imprisonment. A parent has the right physically to chastise his child, and he may, if he wishes, allow a schoolmaster the same right.

What is a guardian?

A person who acts as a parent and has the same authority. A guardian may be appointed by parents in case they die at an early age. A child may also be put under the guardianship of the local authorities if he has no parents or guardian, or if they are prevented by illness or other circumstances from carrying out their duties to the child. A person under 21 can be made a Ward of Court, which means that he is placed under the guardianship of a person appointed by the Court, on matters of education (which school he should attend), where he should live, and general matters of welfare.

What does 'in need of care or protection' mean?

If local authorities hear that a child may be in need of care or protection they first make inquiries about the circumstances of the child's life. If they think that they should help the child they may bring it to the notice of the Juvenile Court. Briefly, a child or young person (up to 14) who is considered to be in this category is one *(a)* without parent or guardian, *(b)* whose parent or guardian is not exercising proper care, *(c)* who is falling in with bad associates, or exposed to moral danger, or beyond control, *(d)* being ill-treated or neglected in a manner likely to cause unnecessary suffering or ill-health. In these cases the Court may send a child to a children's home and perhaps later to foster parents.

What is the definition of foster parents?

These are people – usually married couples – who take children not in the care of their parents into their homes and treat them as their own family. Foster parents may care for a child for a month or for the whole of their school life. They are paid for doing this, although it is doubtful that the amount would ever cover the costs involved.

Which parent has the right to direct a child's religious education?

Under the law of the Church, the godparents have the duty of caring for the child's religious education, but in secular law (non-religious law) the father has the right to have his child brought up in his own religion, although the welfare of the child would be the first consideration if the mother could prove to a Court that bringing the child up in the father's religion would be harmful. Of course, there is nothing in the law to enforce any religious instruction at all.

What action would the Court take if a child is not sent to school?

An order would be made which, if disobeyed, may be treated as contempt of Court, with the penalties of fine or imprisonment. All children must receive education from 5 to 15 years of age. It is hoped to raise this limit to 16 when new buildings can be erected and more teachers recruited. If the authorities consider a parent to be fit to teach his or her child they may, on occasion, permit education of the child at home.

WILLS AND TESTAMENTS

What is the definition of a will?

A will is a written statement of the instructions of the testator (the person who makes the will) regarding the disposal of everything he owns after his death.

What is the purpose of a will?

Its purpose is to give legal and indisputable effect to the testator's instructions regarding his estate. Estate in this case means money, property, personal effects – all that a person owns.

What form must a will take?

Normally a will must be a written document. It can be in the handwriting of a friend or solicitor, or it may be typewritten. It may be written on any surface, such as paper, parchment, cloth – a will has even been written on an eggshell! Scottish law differs slightly in its requirements: it states that if a person writes a will in his own handwriting it need not necessarily be witnessed to be legally effective.

A will must be witnessed in England by two people who must both be present at the time the will is signed by the testator.

Anyone over 21 years of age and in good mental health can witness a will as long as they do not receive any benefit from the will.

It is not necessary to employ a solicitor to draw up a will, providing it is done in the proper way. Will forms (useful but not obligatory) can be obtained at most newsagents and stationers, but the best course is to instruct a solicitor – the legal profession makes a lot of money out of the mistakes of people who have tried to make their own wills!

A will may be made by word of mouth by members of the Forces about to go on active service. Some years ago a young soldier was leaving his home by train. As the train drew out of the station he shouted: 'If anything should happen to me I leave everything to Margaret!' He was killed, the will was held to be valid, and his sister Margaret received his estate.

Where must one sign a will?

At the foot of each page and at the end of the will. If one signs anywhere else, everything after the signature is invalid.

What is a codicil?

A codicil usually reads: 'This is the first [second, etc.] codicil to my will made on the ..... I hereby revoke the bequest made in paragraph three of my will and in place thereof give and bequeath ..... to .....' A Codicil is an addition made after the will is completed or an alteration to an existing will made without destroying or defacing the original. Again, you are best advised to instruct a solicitor.

Should any legal terms be used in the making of a will?

Legal terms should not be used by the ordinary person, as their meaning can be misunderstood; this also applies to abbreviations, semicolons, etc. It is preferable that the will is written as simply as possible. If a person makes his own will he should avoid using legal terms. The will should be written simply, using as few punctuation marks and abbreviations as possible.

Is there a minimum age for making a will?

The minimum age for making a will is 21 years, except for soldiers, airmen and sailors (soldiers and airmen who are on active service and sailors who are actually at sea), who can make a will under the age of 21 years.

If money or property is left to a minor, the executors will act as trustees until the minor becomes 21 years of age. In such a case a minor does not actually own the property until he comes of age. This means that he cannot state what should be done with it if he should die before he attains his majority. Sometimes, though, the term 'of age' may mean 21, 25, 30 – in fact any age, according to the wishes of the testator.

A young man of perhaps 19, who has built up a successful business in his own name, cannot make a will, even though he may have no parents. If he dies his property is disposed of according to the laws of intestacy.

How is a will revoked and why?

A will is revoked (cancelled) when it is destroyed by the person who has made it. It is preferable to destroy a will by tearing it up into small pieces or burning it. A line drawn through a will does not cancel it. If a will is accidentally destroyed it is not revoked. It can also be revoked by the making of a later will, provided all the property mentioned in the previous will is mentioned again in the later one. When one revokes a will by making another, the previous will should be mentioned by inserting the phrase, 'I hereby revoke all previous wills and codicils.'

A will made by a person before marriage is revoked by his or her marriage, providing that the will was not made obviously with the marriage in mind. This is often a point that people forget, and it can cause hardship on the death of the person who has made the will, as the property will be disposed of as though no will has been made.

What are executors and what are their duties?

An executor is a person put in charge of the estate (his authority is written into the will) after the testator's death, to ensure that his wishes are carried out. Executors can be beneficiaries in the will. If none are appointed the beneficiary would have to apply for what are called 'Letters of Administration with the will annexed', to prove that he or she is entitled to take charge of the estate. This process may take some time, as the person will have to obtain a bond from an insurance company (or friends) which will guarantee that the estate will be administered fairly. Even a widow who may receive all her husband's property must do this.

Should a copy of a will be made?

A will is usually lodged in a safe place, at a bank or with a solicitor, so that it is not usually necessary to make a copy. A bank is probably preferable – one may wish to change solicitors occasionally!

Does the amount of money or property make a difference to the procedure of making a will?

No, although a complex will allows more room for mistakes and ambiguities.

What are the standard charges for making a will?

A solicitor charges according to the

length and complexity of a will; a fair charge made for a simple will leaving everything to one beneficiary would be two or three guineas.

How does one prove a will?

No one can benefit under a will until it has been proved, except in the case of very small estates of under £200. The larger the estate the longer the will takes to prove, as inquiries will have to be made about the various forms of assets (shares, savings certificates, etc.) of the estate.

One can go to a solicitor and put the will in his hands to prove, or one can go personally to the District Probate Registry (the principal one is at Somerset House) where the Personal Application Department will set in motion the machinery for proving the will. Proving a will entails filing it at Somerset House together with certain official forms and a detailed statement of all the assets of the estate, and payment of registration fees. You will then be told how much estate duty has to be paid. At the present time none is payable if the net estate is under £4,000. Above

99

this there is a sliding scale starting at I per cent and rising to 80 per cent for millionaires.

When duty has been paid and the Probate Registrar is satisfied, a probate of the will is issued to the executors authorising them to carry out the testator's wishes, and the will is officially filed as a public document, and can then be inspected by anyone on payment of a small fee.

The time taken to prove a will can sometimes cause hardship to the beneficiary, who is often the wife of the testator. She will not be able to draw on her late husband's bank account until it is proved. It is often advisable to take out a small insurance cover in the wife's name to overcome this difficulty, or to have a joint banking account.

If relatives consider that a will is unfair, can they upset it?

A will cannot be changed unless *dependent* relatives consider they have been left insufficient money or property. They can then claim in court under the Family Provisions Inheritance Act. If, for instance, a person

The will is read to the family

gave a home to his aunt for a number of years without receiving payment, and when she died it was found that she had left all her money to a dogs' home, there would be no case for a claim because he had not been in any way dependent upon her. But if a wife or her dependent children are cut out of her husband's will, she may claim. The court case *must* be started within six months of the date on which probate is granted.

The only other way in which a relative can attack a will is by proving that someone used undue influence on the testator when the will was made, or the testator was not then of sound mind.

Can a creditor prove a will if no executors have been appointed?

Yes, he can apply for Letters of Administration with the will annexed to show that nobody else is interested in proving it.

Usually the residuary legatee (the person to whom the residue of the estate – often the largest portion – is left) proves the will in such circumstances.

How is an estate distributed on the intestacy of a husband?

The first £5,000 goes to the widow, with the personal effects (furniture, car, etc.) She also receives a life interest in half the residue. The children of the testator receive the other half of the residue between them. If there is no widow the children take all. If there is no widow or children, the estate goes to the testator's parents, or if they are not living to his brothers and sisters (equally shared), and so on down the family line. If there are no relatives the estate belongs to the Crown.

How is a search for beneficiaries or, in a case of intestacy, relatives, made?

By advertisement in the London Gazette and newspapers published in the area in which the beneficiary was thought to live. For example, if a testator's brother (who was a beneficiary) lived in Australia and could not be found, the estate would be held in trust until he was located or until his death had been finally proved. There are, incidentally, many millions of pounds in Britain waiting to be claimed.

Here is a specimen of a simple will. Its clear and concise terms make it simple for anyone to follow.

This is the last will and testament of me John Smith, of Number Seven, Heathwood Road, Stapleton, in the County of Yorkshire, Mechanic, made this twentieth day of February one thousand nine hundred and sixty three.

1. I hereby revoke all Wills and codicils made by me at any time heretofore. I appoint my wife, Mary Smith, and James Hill, of Winton Road, Stapleton, aforesaid, Joiner, to be my executors, and direct that all my debts and funeral expenses shall be paid as soon as conveniently may be after my decease.

2. I give and bequeath unto my Son, Alan Smith, the sum of three hundred pounds (free of duty), unto my daughter, Joan Smith, my freehold dwelling house at 53, Hazel Crescent, Branton (free of duty), and all the remainder of my property to my said wife Mary Smith absolutely.

Signed by the Testator
in our presence and attested
by us in the presence of him
and of each other   JOHN SMITH

CLIVE ROACH,	MICHAEL GALE,
Hayward Road,	St John Street,
Richmond,	Coverthwaite,
fitter.	driver.

BUYING BUSINESS AND BANKRUPTCY

Has a buyer any redress for defects in new goods bought on hire purchase?

The fact that the goods are bought on hire purchase does not in any way affect the basic conditions upon which they have been sold. The buyer has the same warranty whether he pays outright or on H.P. He receives a warranty for 'quiet possession' of the goods (i.e. a guarantee that nobody will take them away from him without due cause), and the warranty also undertakes that the goods are free from defects, even if no written guarantee accompanies them. If the buyer is not satisfied that the goods comply with these conditions he can return them. Buying on H.P. does not interfere with the usual procedure if one buys faulty goods.

If a purchase is later found to be stolen, may the buyer keep it?

A buyer receives no better title to the goods than the title of the person who sold them. If the man who sold them did not own them, the buyer also does not own them. There is, however, one main exception. If the goods were sold in 'market overt', that is in an open market such as a country market place, or Petticoat Lane, then under old common law the buyer would have more chance of keeping them – as long as he did not know they were stolen, of course.

If goods are found to be stolen the buyer must give them up to the Police or to the original owner. The person who sold the goods will have to refund the price, or he may be sued for fraud, misrepresentation, or breach of the warranty that the buyer would have quiet possession of the goods.

Must goods be described accurately?

Goods must be reasonably within the description given of them. But there are a number of snags. If a car, for example, is described as a 100 m.p.h. vehicle, able to travel thirty miles to the gallon, it would be useless to complain if it did not perform exactly as described. But if the description is blatantly false – if knives described as stainless steel turn out to be of inferior metal – then one has a legitimate complaint.

Stolen goods on a stall in Petticoat Lane

If a dress is stated to be 'pure silk' then it must be of that material, but if it is simply labelled 'silk' then it may be a mixture (the proportions of which are laid down by law) of perhaps rayon and silk.

If goods are sold 'as per sample' then they must be of the same quality as the sample.

In a recent case a ship was sold described as 'copper fastened', but was sold 'with all faults'. It was found to be fastened by an inferior method, and it was held that the seller was not protected by the stipulation 'with all faults', having in fact sold the ship as 'copper fastened with all faults' which was an inaccurate description.

Must a promised delivery date be kept, and if it is not, can the potential buyer do anything about it?

He can cancel the order, and if the delivery date was specified in the contract and is very much delayed, causing serious inconvenience, the buyer can also take proceedings against the seller for non-performance of his contract.

A magazine publisher ordered a large quantity of special paper to print an issue of his journal. The supplier agreed to deliver the paper by a certain date. He failed to do so, the magazine could not be published, and the publisher lost several thousand pounds. The supplier had to pay up.

Conversely, when a potential buyer has ordered an item, he has entered into a binding agreement to accept it. This agreement is not often enforced in everyday purchases.

Who is responsible for bad food sold over the counter?

The person who actually sells the food is usually responsible, but if the food is sold in a container, preventing the grocer from examining it, then, in certain circumstances, he may be able to make his supplier responsible. Bear in mind that a buyer is always entitled to assume that any foodstuffs on sale are fit for consumption.

If a radio in a shop is marked by mistake at £20, is the shopkeeper bound to sell it to a customer at that price?

No. Priced goods in a shop window – or on the shelves – do not comprise an offer

Is the fishmonger responsible if he sells bad fish?

to sell them at that price, they are merely an invitation to the public to buy. If a shopkeeper puts a blouse in his window and marks it at 39s 11d, he has not stated that he will sell it to anyone who comes into the shop, he has merely invited the public in to trade. He need not sell any of his goods to a shopper if he does not wish to do so.

Must goods weigh as marked?

Yes. It is illegal to give less than the specified weight, and surprisingly, it is also illegal to give overweight. If a person orders a hundredweight of coal, then he is entitled to that, no more, no less, although complaints about overweight are few and far between!

If a shopkeeper states that an item, a certain type of nail, for example, will carry a certain weight or do a specific job, is he responsible for a possible failure?

Yes. If a buyer asks the shopkeeper's advice, he implies that he is relying on the shopkeeper's superior knowledge and experience. If the shopkeeper chooses to advise the customer, then he is bound by that advice.

In what circumstances can a finance company take back goods bought on hire purchase?

In the case of small hire purchase contracts – radio, washing machine, carpet, etc. – the goods may be reclaimed by the finance company if the hirer fails to pay an instalment within a specified number of days (sometimes seven) or if he becomes bankrupt, or has a distress warrant served against him. Then the owner (usually a finance company) may terminate the hiring and repossess his goods.

He may not do so, however, if the hire purchaser has paid one-third of the price plus H.P. charges. Then the goods may not be taken away from him without a court order; if payments temporarily fall behind the finance company cannot just walk in and reclaim the goods.

In the case of contracts involving more than £300 the powers of the finance company may be greater, so always check the small print.

The laws regarding hire purchase are in a fluid state at the moment, and further changes in the law for the greater protection of the public may soon be made.

**If goods that are being bought on hire pur-
chase are later damaged, must the fact be
reported to the finance company?**

Most H.P. agreements include a clause
stating that the hirer must keep the goods
in reasonable order, and that if they are
lost or completely destroyed he must pay
the balance of the hire purchase money, but
it is not usual to inform the company of
damage except in the case of a motor car
or other large item, when a clause is often
found binding the hirer to inform the
company of serious damage.

**When the hire purchase money on a car has
been paid, why does one often have to pay
an additional ten shillings?**

The last clause of many agreements
states that after all the instalments have
been paid the hirer has the option (but
shall not be bound) to buy the car outright
for a nominal sum. This is just a legal point
which officially sets the seal on the deal.

Is an I.O.U. recognised in court?

An I.O.U. is a document which acknowledges a debt in writing. It is almost always
recognised as evidence by the Court.

What is the object of a stamp on a receipt?

It is merely another form of revenue for the Treasury. Receipts for over £2 must still have a 2d stamp on them, although many people think that this law was changed a few years ago. The actual change related to cheques, which are now considered a form of receipt (or evidence of payment) even though not endorsed by the recipient. Receipts are not now usually sent for payments by cheque except on request.

A receipt is no less valid if it has no stamp on it, but the person who has given the receipt may get into trouble for evading a legitimate tax.

Many other documents are required to be stamped; all contracts, deeds transferring land for more than £3,500, mortgages of land, insurance policies and a host of other documents must have a stamp affixed to them.

What is the purpose of a small business-man forming a limited company?

A limited company is, as its title implies, a company of limited liability. This means that if, say, it is formed with a hundred shares at £1 each, then its share capital is £100. The shares are issued either for cash or its equivalent value. If the business fails and closes down, the shareholders only lose the amounts they paid for their shares, which is a protection against the failure of a small business encroaching on the private pockets of its directors. But the directors may be personally liable if they have broken the law in running the company. Of course, it also limits the purchasing power of a company. If you have formed a new transport company with a share capital of £100, you would not find many people willing to sell you a £2,000 motor lorry on credit!

On the other hand several of the biggest companies in Britain are '£100 companies' who have never bothered to increase their share capital, and yet deal in several million pounds worth of goods every year.

What is the difference between a private and public company?

A private company is one which by its articles restricts the right to transfer its shares, limits the number of its members who may be shareholders to fifty (exclusive of past and present employees of the company) and prohibits any invitation to the public to subscribe for its shares.

Private companies may become public companies, and they very often do. When a private company has developed considerably it sometimes needs to expand still further, but lacks the capital to do so. Then it may be changed into a public company, one which is allowed to 'float' extra share capital (i.e. create extra shares) which are offered to the public.

What is the procedure for forming a private company?

Four main documents must be filed with the Registrar of Companies at 55 City Road, London, E. C. 1, and registration fees and capital duty paid. A Memorandum of Association, normally drawn up by a solicitor, and signed by at least two members of the new company, must be filed.

Then there are the Articles of Association, which regulate the internal affairs of the company. This document must be signed by the same persons who sign the Memorandum. These first two documents are usually presented in the form of one booklet, called the Memorandum and Articles of Association of XYZ Ltd.

The third document which must be filed is the statutory declaration by a solicitor (or a proposed director or company secretary) stating that all the requirements of the Act relating to registration have been fulfilled. This is called the Declaration of Compliance. Finally a statement of the share capital must be filed.

When these have been filed the Registrar will issue a Certificate of Incorporation, and the company may commence business, but should promptly file the notice of its registered office, particulars of its directors and security, and the names and addresses of its shareholders.

What are the costs of forming a private company?

The cost of forming a private company with a nominal share capital of £100, including the printing of the Memorandum and Articles, the filing of all necessary documents, and the making of the company's Seal, would amount to about £35. The solicitor's fees, included in the total figure, would be about £10 – 12. Some business firms specialise in providing ready-made companies at low cost.

What is bankruptcy?

Bankruptcy is the condition of a private person whose liabilities exceed his assets and who has committed an act of bankruptcy.

There are various acts of bankruptcy: for instance, a person who has been told to comply with a court order for the payment of a debt within twenty-one days, and fails to do so because he has no money. By failing, he commits an act of bankruptcy upon which a petition can be based by the creditor.

An act of bankruptcy may also be made by a person who is unable to pay his debts, and whose personal possessions are of less value than his debts, saying to his creditors: 'I cannot pay you, but here are my own goods. Share them out between you.' A person may file his own declaration of his inability to pay his debts, attend the public examination, and be declared bankrupt by the court.

Bankruptcy applies only to private individuals. A limited company unable to settle its debts goes into what is known as voluntary or compulsory liquidation. This state is often called the 'winding up' of a company.

A bankrupt person cannot obtain goods on credit, nor can he hold a bank account. Virtually all his goods belong to the trustee in bankruptcy, who is an official of the Court appointed to administer his goods and financial affairs. All his earnings must be declared, with a view to using part of them to pay back his debts if he wishes a future discharge from bankruptcy.

Can the Court seize the possessions of a bankrupt's wife?

If they are her own goods they cannot be taken by her husband's creditors. Gifts given to her by her husband usually two years before the bankruptcy cannot be taken, if it cannot be proved that they were given to her with intent to defraud the creditors.

How can a bankrupt person get a discharge?

He can apply for discharge at any time after the public examination has been concluded, but the Court is never bound either to refuse or to grant a discharge outright. Often a Court finds that it cannot grant an immediate unconditional discharge, but makes one of the following orders. It may either refuse a discharge, or suspend it for a period that it thinks proper, or suspend it until ten shillings in the pound has been paid off the debts. At other times it may grant a discharge providing the bankrupt agrees to be responsible for paying off the balance of the debts as soon as he can possibly do so.

What is a bailiff?

He is an officer of the court, more usually of a County Court. His primary function is the enforcement of court orders, and he helps in the recovery of possession of property, goods and chattels, the recovery of debts, etc.

Can one be imprisoned for debt?

Contrary to popular belief one cannot be imprisoned for debt today. But a debtor can be imprisoned for contempt of court: i.e. refusing to comply with a court order which

The bailiff

demands the payment of a debt when the debtor is known to have enough money to pay.

Hire purchase agreements

All too often, when a person is presented with a hire purchase agreement at a shop, he is so eager to take his newly acquired property home quickly that in the excitement he does not read the 'small print' of the agreement. Here is a typically fair agreement that you may meet when buying a radio or television set on hire purchase. This form of agreement has been set out by the Radio and Television Retailers' Association.

This Agreement is made this 1st day of January 1963 between A. F. Hunt Ltd., of 26 High Road Packwell, Herts. hereinafter called the owner and John Smith of 20 Redding Street Packwell, Herts. hereinafter called the hirer.

WHEREBY it is agreed as follows:

General 1. The initial payment (if any) shown in the Schedule hereto having been made, the owner will let out, and the hirer will take, the goods specified in the Schedule hereto (hereinafter called the goods) on hire upon the terms hereinafter appearing, until the hiring is duly terminated or the hirer buys the goods.

Hire Rent 2. The hirer shall pay to the dealer by way of hire rent the periodic instalments set out in the said Schedule at the times there stated until the Hire Purchase Price stated in the said Schedule (hereinafter called the Hire Purchase Price) has been paid by such instalments (after giving credit for the said initial payment, if any).

Installation charges 3. Where an installation charge is referred to in the said Schedule, the owner shall install the goods and the hirer shall pay such charge as part of the Hire Purchase Price.

Option to purchase property in goods 4. When the hirer has paid the Hire Purchase Price in full he may purchase the goods, and the owner shall sell the goods to him, but until such payment and purchase the goods shall be the sole property of the owner. No further sum shall be payable on such purchase.

Safe custody of goods 5. The hirer shall not, during the hiring, part with possession of, or deal with the goods, nor attempt so to do, and shall keep the goods at his address as stated at the head of this agreement, unless the owner gives permission in writing (which is not to be unreasonably refused) to remove them.

Care of goods 6. The hirer shall, throughout the hiring, and until the goods have been bought by him or returned to the owner, keep the goods safe from loss or damage by fire or any other cause and in good repair, but the hirer shall not himself tamper with or adjust or repair the goods, nor allow any other person to do so, save a competent radio or electronic engineer.

Insurance 7. The hirer shall, throughout the hiring, and until the goods have been bought by him or returned to the owner, keep the goods insured for the Hire Purchase Price, in the name of the owner (or, if the owner permits, in the joint names of the owner and the hirer) against loss or damage to the goods by fire, storm, flood, burglary and theft, with an Insurance Company approved by the owner, and shall, on demand, produce to the owner or his authorised agent the policy and premium receipt.

Inspection 8. The hirer shall permit the owner and his servants or agents to inspect the goods at all reasonable times and shall permit them to enter upon any premises under his control for this purpose.

Termination of hiring by hirer 9. The hirer may put an end to the hiring in accordance with the Statutory Notice under the Hire Purchase Acts which is printed below and is incorporated in this agreement. The hirer shall have no other right to determine the hiring (except by purchasing the goods on payment of the Hire Purchase Price).

Termination by owner 10. (*a*) If the hirer either fails for seven days to make any payment stipulated for in this agreement, or commits any other breach of this agreement, or commits any act of bankruptcy, or permits any judgment against him to remain unsatisfied for seven days, or if any distress or execution is levied or threatened upon the goods or upon the property of the hirer or at the premises in which the goods are kept, the owner may in any such case, either without prior notice or (in his discretion) by written notice delivered to the hirer or sent by post to his last known address, forthwith terminate the hiring. Thereupon the owner shall be entitled to immediate possession of the goods, which shall not thereafter

127

be in the hirer's possession with the owner's consent, and the owner may (subject to the Hire Purchase Acts 1938-54) retake the goods.

(b) If the hiring is terminated under this clause, the hirer shall pay to the owner the arrears of hire rent due at the date of termination and such further sum as may be necessary to make the sums paid by the hirer equal to the sum specified in paragraph 2 of the first part of the statutory notice printed below (or, if no sum is specified, to half the Hire Purchase Price).

Termination General

11. The termination of the hiring by either the owner or the hirer shall not prejudice or affect any right of the owner to recover any arrears of hire rent due at such termination or any damages for breach of this agreement and no sum paid to the owner shall be repayable by reason of such termination.

Loss or destruction of goods

12 (a) If the hirer parts with possession of the goods (before having paid the Hire Purchase Price) he shall forthwith pay the balance of the Hire Purchase Price then outstanding to the owner.

(b) If the goods are destroyed or lost before the hirer has paid the Hire Purchase Price, the hirer shall, within one month, pay to the owner the balance of the Hire Purchase Price then outstanding, less a discount of $2\frac{1}{2}\%$ per annum upon the whole of such balance for the period during which instalments would have been payable. Upon such payment the hirer shall be entitled to the benefit of any sum received or receivable under the policy of insurance on the goods.

Conditions and warranties 13 (*a*) The goods are supplied subject to the warranties and conditions implied by section 8 (1) of the Hire Purchase Act 1938 and to no other conditions or warranties, expressed or implied. The hirer hereby agrees and declares that he has examined the goods and found them free from defect.

(*b*) It is agreed and declared that the goods are not supplied subject to any condition or warranty that they are fit for any purpose. This shall not prejudice any rights which the hirer may acquire under any manufacturer's guarantee.

Indulgence 14. If the owner grants any time or other indulgence to the hirer or delays in enforcing his rights, this shall not amount to a waiver by the owner of his rights or of any breach of this agreement by the hirer and

Payments

No Assignment

shall not prevent the owner thereafter relying upon his strict rights
under this agreement without notice.
15. Payments are to be made at the
owner's premises. If the hirer pays
by post, he does so at his own risk.
16. The hirer may not assign this
agreement.

SCHEDULE

Serial No.	Trade Name or Description of Goods	Price for which goods can be bought for cash				
089078	Explorer Radio	£ 23	s. 12	d. 6	Total cash price(bt.fwd.)	£ 23 s. 12 d. 6
					* Hire purchase charges	1 10 0
					Installation charges	
					HIRE PUR-CHASE PRICE	25 2 6
					Less, initial payment (if any)	9 2 6
	Total Cash Price (carry forward)	23	12	6	BALANCE payable by hirer	16 0 0

INSTALMENTS. The balance of the Hire Purchase Price shall be paid by TWELVE (12) monthly instalments of £1 6s 8d each †(and one instalment of £ . . . s . . . d. The first instalment shall be paid on 30th FEBRUARY 1963 and each subsequent instalment shall be paid on the . . . . . . day of each succeeding week/month.

* Calculated on Cash Price less initial payment
† If necessary

The attractions of hire purchase

STATUTORY NOTICE

Right of Hirer to terminate Agreement.

1. The Hirer may put an end to this agreement by giving notice of termination in writing to any person who is entitled to collect or receive the hire rent.

* Here insert one half of cash price and hire purchase charges plus whole of installation charges (see general note 5)

2. He must then pay any instalments which are in arrear at the time when he gives notice. If, when he has paid those instalments, the total amount which he has paid under the agreement is less than £12 13s 3d he must also pay enough to make up that sum.

3. If the goods have been damaged owing to the hirer having failed to take reasonable care of them, the owner may sue him for the amount of damages unless that amount can be agreed between the hirer and the owner.

4. The hirer should see whether this agreement contains provisions allowing him to put an end to the agreement on terms more favourable to him than those just mentioned. If it does, he may put an end to the agreement on those terms.

Restriction of Owner's right to recover goods.

*Here insert one-third of cash price and hire purchase charges, plus whole of instalation charges (see general note 5)

1. [After * £8 7s 6d has been paid, then], unless the hirer has himself put an end to the agreement, the owner of the goods cannot take them back from the hirer without the hirer's consent unless the owner obtains an order of the Court.

2. If the owner applies to the Court for such an order, the Court may if it thinks it just to do so, allow the hirer to keep either:

(*a*) the whole of the goods, on condition that the hirer pays the balance of the price in the manner ordered by the Court; or

(*b*) a fair proportion of the goods having regard to what the hirer has already paid.

If the agreement is a 'further' agreement within the meaning of sec. 15 of the Hire Purchase Act, the words in square brackets should be omitted.

IN WITNESS of this agreement the hirer and the owner have hereunto set their hands.

Signed by the hirer in the presence of
Signature of first witness
Address
Occupation

Signature of second witness
(Scotland only)
Address
Occupation
Signature of hirer
Date
Place where signed
(Scotland only)
Signed by the owner
Date

N.B. The agreement is not complete
or binding until accepted and signed
by the owner.

*This form of agreement is copyright
by the Radio and Television Retailers'
Association and is available to members
only.*

The terms of agreement for larger items
are similar in general stipulations, but usually are for goods costing more than the
figure below which the hirer (purchaser)
is protected by the Hire Purchase Act,
which says that if goods cost under £300
the owner (seller) cannot take them back
against the hirer's will, if he has paid off
more than a third of the price.

Here is the form of agreement that a car
buyer will fill in if he hire purchases his
vehicle through the United Dominions Trust

(Commercial) Ltd.: it is scrupulously fair, and is widely used throughout the country.

After detailing the price, description of the car, and the hire purchaser's address, the agreement has the Statutory notice for goods under £300, which reads as follows:

NOTICE

(Applicable and to be completed only if the hire purchase price does not exceed £300)

Right of Hirer to Terminate Agreement

1. The hirer may put an end to this Agreement by giving notice of termination in writing to any person who is entitled to collect or receive the hire rent.

2. He must then pay any instalments which are in arrear at the time when he gives notice. If, when he has paid those instalments, the total amount which he has paid under the Agreement is less than £* : : he must also pay enough to make up that sum.

3. If the goods have been damaged owing to the Hirer having failed to take reasonable care of them, the Owner may sue him for the amount of the damage unless that amount can be agreed between the Hirer and the Owner.

4. The Hirer should see whether this Agreement contains provisions allowing him to put an end to the Agreement on terms more favourable to him than those just mentioned. If it does, he may put an end to the Agreement on those terms.

Restriction of Owner's Right to Recover Goods

1. After £† : : has been paid, then, unless the Hirer has himself put an end to the Agreement, the Owner of the goods cannot take them back from the Hirer without the Hirer's consent unless the Owner obtains an Order of the Court.

2. If the Owner applies to the Court for such an Order, the Court may, if the Court thinks it just to do so, allow the Hirer to keep either —

(a) the whole of the goods, on condition that the Hirer pays the balance of the price in the manner ordered by the Court; or

(b) a fair proportion of the goods having regard to what the Hirer has already paid.

* Insert one-half of the Hire Purchase Price

† Insert one-third of the Hire Purchase Price.

SIGNATURE OF PARTIES

(i) HIRER

In signing this agreement the Hirer acknowledges that before he signed it

(a) He had seen a written statement of the cash price of the goods which corresponded exactly with that shown in the Schedule above;

(b) His attention had been drawn to the provisions of clause (2) overleaf and it had been made clear to him that the effect of that clause was to exclude any warranty by the Owner that the goods were fit for any particular purpose; and

(c) He had examined the goods and satisfied himself that they were in good order and condition.

Witness

Address   Signature of Hirer

(ii)

Signature of Owner
                    p.p. UNITED DOMINIONS
                    TRUST (COMMERCIAL)
                            LIMITED

Witness . . . .

Address . . . .

BY THIS AGREEMENT made between UNITED DOMINIONS TRUST (COMMERCIAL) LIMITED of United Dominions House Eastcheap, London, E.C. 3 (hereinafter called 'the Owner') of the one part and Hirer named in the Schedule hereto (hereinafter called 'the goods') upon the terms set out below and in the Schedule (which forms part of this agreement).

Terms 1. The hiring shall begin on the date specified in the Schedule and unless determined by the Hirer or by the Owner as hereinafter provided shall continue for the period of hire specified in the Schedule. The hirer shall upon the making of this agreement pay the initial instalment of rent specified in the Schedule and shall punctually pay the several instalments of the balance of hire as set out in the Schedule on the dates therein provided. The Hirer shall pay interest at the rate of 8% per annum on all overdue instalments until payment thereof and the rights of the Owner hereunder shall not in any way be affected by any time or other indulgence that the Owner may see fit to grant to the Hirer. Each and every Hirer party hereto shall be severally as well as jointly liable to the Owner for the due performance and observance of all the terms of this agreement.

2. The Hirer's acceptance of delivery of the goods shall be conclusive that he has examined the goods and found them to be complete and in good order and condition and in every way satisfactory to him. Except as provided by the Hire Purchase Acts 1938 and 1954, the Owner gives no warranty as to the state or quality of the goods and, save as aforesaid, any warranty as to description, repair, quality or fitness for any purpose is hereby excluded. The Owner shall not be liable for any delay in delivery to the Hirer of the goods which shall be at the risk of the Hirer from the time of purchase by the Owner.

3. The Hirer shall forthwith at his own expensure insure the goods in a reputable office comprehensively against all usual risks including loss or damage by fire, theft and accident and shall keep them so insured during the currency of this agreement. Alternatively, the Hirer shall insure the goods in such office and against such risks and generally in such form as the Owner may reasonably require

him to do. In either event, the Hirer will upon request at any time produce to the Owner the policy and the receipt for the current year's premium and should the Hirer fail to do so, the Owner shall be entitled at the Hirer's expense to insure the goods and keep them so insured during the currency of this agreement and the Hirer will pay to the Owner on demand any sums expended by the Owner in so doing. Should the Hirer by exercising the option to purchase contained in this agreement become the owner of the goods during the currency of any policy of insurance thus taken out by the Owner, the Owner will, as the case may be, either at the expense of the Hirer and subject to any necessary consents of the insurers transfer to the Hirer the benefit of any such policy or surrender the policy to the insurers and credit the Hirer with any rebate of premium obtainable thereon.

4. The Hirer shall notify his insurers that the goods are the property of the Owner and shall request his insurers to endorse a note of such ownership on any policy taken out by him to cover them. Should the goods be lost or sustain serious dam-

age the Hirer shall notify the Owner of the fact and shall, if the Owner calls upon him to do so, forthwith at his own expense assign to the Owner all rights, claims and benefits under any such policy. All moneys payable under any such policy in respect of loss of or damage to the goods (other than moneys payable to repairers) shall in any event be paid by the insurers to the Owners and the Hirer hereby irrevocably authorises the Owner to give a good discharge to the insurers therefor. If the owner shall at any time agree to any modification or restriction in the insurance cover herein provided for, or if for any other reason the goods shall not be fully covered by insurance, the Hirer shall indemnify the Owner against any loss which the Owner may sustain as a consequence.

5. During the currency of this agreement the Hirer shall keep the goods in his own possession and shall not take them out of the United Kingdom without the previous consent in writing of the Owner and shall maintain the goods in proper repair and in good and serviceable condition (making good all damage thereto whether or not occasioned by his own act or default) and shall not

use or permit to be used for any purpose for which they are not designed or reasonably suitable and shall not hold himself out as owner of the goods nor sell, offer for sale, assign or charge the goods or the benefit of this agreement nor create any lien on the goods or pledge the Owner's credit either for repairs thereto or otherwise and shall not interfere or allow any interference with any identification marks thereon or attempt to do any of these things.

6. The goods are and shall remain the property of the Owner unless and until the Hirer exercises the option to purchase contained in this agreement after having become entitled to do so. All replacements and renewals of components parts and accessories and all additions and alterations forming an integral part of the goods made during the currency of this agreement shall be deemed to form part of the goods. The Hirer will at all times allow the Owner reasonable facilities for inspecting the goods and access for this purpose to any premises in or upon which the goods may be. The Hirer shall punctually pay all rent, rates, taxes and outgoings in connection with any premises in or upon which the goods may be

for the time being and if required to do so shall produce to the Owner receipts for such payments.

7. During the currency of this agreement, the Hirer shall not use or permit the goods to be used in contravention of any statute or regulations for the time being in force or otherwise in any way contrary to law and shall pay any licence duties, fees and registration charges payable in respect of the goods, and, if any such liability shall be discharged by the Owner, shall repay the same to the Owner on demand. The Hirer shall pay any costs, damages, losses, charges and expenses incurred by the Owner in collecting arrears of any moneys payable hereunder or in exercising any of the powers contained herein. If the hire-purchase price shewn in the Schedule does not exceed £300 (but not otherwise) the Notice overleaf is to be deemed part of this agreement and, in that event should there be any inconsistency between the terms of such Notice and anything contained elsewhere in this agreement, the terms of the Notice are to prevail.

8. Should the Hirer fail to pay the initial instalment of rent in full at the time when this agreement is made

or to pay any subsequent instalment or other sum payable hereunder in full within ten days after the same shall have become due or if he shall die or have a Receiving Order made against him or be made bankrupt or call any meeting of or make any arrangement or composition with his creditors or if the Hirer being a limited company shall call any meeting of its creditors or be wound up compulsorily or go into voluntary liquidation or have a receiver of any of its assets appointed or if the goods or any part thereof shall be seized under any execution or legal process issued against the Hirer or under any distress for rent or if the Hirer shall fail to observe or fulfil any term of this agreement or shall do or suffer anything whatsoever which in the Owner's opinion bona fide formed upon reasonable grounds will or may have the effect of jeopardising the Owner's right of property in the goods then and in each and every such case the Owner may forthwith and without any notice terminate the hiring; or alternatively, by written notice (either served personally on the Hirer or sent to him by post at his usual or last-known address) forthwith and for all purposes terminate the hiring and this agreement and thereafter the Hirer shall no longer be in possession of the goods with the Owner's consent.

9. Should the hiring be terminated by the Owner under Clause 8 hereof, the Owner may (though not without the consent of the Hirer where the hire-purchase price does not exceed £300 and one-third of such price has been paid) without any notice retake possession of the goods and for this purpose shall be entitled (unless the hire-purchase price of the goods does not exceed £300) freely to enter into and upon any premises occupied by or under the control of the Hirer, and, notwithstanding the termination of the hiring, the Hirer shall be liable for all instalments of rent which shall then be in arrear and unpaid (together with interest thereon until payment at the rate of 8% per annum) and for any other sums then due or thereupon becoming due to the Owner under this agreement. If, however, the hire-purchase price of the goods does not exceed £300 and one-third of such price has been paid, then, unless the Hirer has himself put an end to the agreement, the Owner may not take back the

goods from the Hirer without the Hirer's consent unless the Owner obtains an order of the Court in accordance with the Notice overleaf.

10. The Hirer may at any time terminate the hiring by returning the goods at his own expense and risk to the Owner at such place as shall be appointed by the Owner in a good state of repair and in good working order and condition and with such additions, alterations and improvements as shall have been made thereto without becoming thereby entitled to any credit allowance or set-off in respect of payments previously made and without prejudice to the rights of the Owner in respect of any breach of the Hirer's covenants herein contained.

11. Should the hiring be terminated by the Hirer under Clause 10 or by the Owner under Clause 8 hereof the Hirer shall (save where the hirepurchase price does not exceed £300) forthwith pay to the Owner either (a) such further sum as with the total amount of any instalments previously paid hereunder will an equal two-thirds of the total hiring cost shewn in the Schedule as agreed compensation for the depreciation of

the goods or (*b*) the amount of all instalments and other moneys then already due hereunder, whichever is the greater. Where the hire purchase price does not exceed £300, the Hirer's liability under this clause shall be the same as it would have been had he himself put an end to the agreement in accordance with the Notice overleaf.

12. If and when all instalments and other moneys payable by the Hirer to the Owner under this agreement shall have been duly paid and provided that the Hirer shall not have committed any breach of the provisions of this agreement then the Hirer shall have the option (but shall not be bound) to purchase the goods for the sum of one pound.

CHAPTER SIX

MOTORING

Where can a provisional driving licence be obtained?

A provisional driving licence form (the same one as the ordinary driving licence renewal form D.L.1.) can be obtained from any post office. Answer the appropriate questions, enclose 10s and send it to the local authority. A provisional licence for six months will be returned.

What are the qualifications needed to obtain a full driving licence?

A person must have passed the driving test and must be of a minimum age of 17 years (16 is the minimum age for motor cycles). A driver must not suffer from any disease or physical disability likely to cause danger on the roads. Some of these disabilities are listed: epilepsy, sudden attacks of giddiness or fainting, and mental disorder or defect, or the inability to read (with glasses) a number plate at 25 yards.

Must a vehicle be comprehensively insured?

No; the minimum insurance allowable on a vehicle to be driven on public roads is a 'third party' policy. This covers damage or injury a motorist may inflict on another road user and his car, but the holder of a third party policy will have to pay for his own repairs – and injuries – out of his own pocket. Third party policies are considerably cheaper than comprehensive ones but can sometimes cause the holder hardship.

What is a Road Fund Licence?

Commonly called car tax, this is a sum payable to local authorities, and was originally intended for the upkeep of the roads. For a private car the duty is £15 a year except in the case of cars registered before January 1st, 1947, when it is £10 15s 0d and £12 10s 0d for cars not exceeding 6 h.p. and 7 h.p. respectively. If you elect to pay every four months the tax (for a modern car) is £5 10s 0d payable three times a year. The licence disc must be displayed on the windscreen of the car.

What are the responsibilities of a driving instructor (official or private) when accompanying a learner driver who commits an offence?

If an instructor could reasonably prevent

the offence (i.e. exceeding the speed limit, or driving through stoplights) they may both be responsible – the pupil for an offence under the Road Traffic Act and the instructor for aiding and abetting. If the pupil merely commits an error of driving which involves them in an accident, then he alone is responsible.

What is the position of an owner who allows his car to be driven by a friend who then is involved in an accident?

Firstly, the owner should let a friend drive his car only if his (the owner's) insurance policy states that any driver may use the car. Many insurance policies specify that the owner only may drive – in which case any accident that an uninsured friend may have, will bring charges against both of them.

From the point of view of the insurance any claim will be paid by the company with whom the owner has a policy, but in certain circumstances the law may charge the driver with an offence under the Road Traffic Acts and the owner for aiding and abetting.

An L driver involved in an accident

If a dog runs out of a front garden and damages a moving car is the owner of the dog liable?

No, not unless it can be proved that the dog's owner was negligent in handling his pet, or that he enticed it across the road in the path of an oncoming car. The owner of a cat would be held even less responsible for his pet's actions.

Should a motorist report to the police after accidentally running down and killing a cat or a dog?

He need not report after running over a cat, but must if he kills or injures a dog.

Must the Police be contacted after all accidents?

Basically, a driver must stop and report to the Police after any accident involving personal injury (or possible injury) to another person, or to an animal. If a driver damages another vehicle, however, he need only stop and exchange information – his name and address, the name and address of the owner of the car and the number of the car – with the driver of the other vehicle.

Personal injury means even the slightest of cuts, or a small bruise. These may develop into serious injuries in time, and the Police wish to know about them.

If a driver damages property (i.e. a fence, wall, gate, etc.) he need not report at all. But if the car can be traced by the owner of the damaged property, the driver may be sued for damages.

Is it permissible to drive a car or caravan off the road on to near-by land for a meal or to sleep the night?

A vehicle may be parked on land up to a distance of 15 yards from the verge only if it does not infringe the law of trespass or any local regulation. If you intend to stay the night it is in any case a wise precaution to ask permission of the Police or local authority, in case any by-laws are broken.

What are the speed limits for goods vehicles?

A goods vehicle is restricted to 30 m.p.h. If it tows a trailer the limit is 20 m.p.h. For the purpose of limiting speeds a goods

A crowd gathers as the police arrive on the scene

vehicle is described as 'a vehicle which is constructed or adapted for the carriage of goods or burden of any description.' Vehicles designed to carry more than 7 passengers are limited to 40 m.p.h. and invalid carriages are restricted to 20 m.p.h.

Under a normal comprehensive policy is an owner-driver's wife covered for personal injury and damage to clothing if she and her husband are involved in an accident which is proved to be his fault?

No. A normal policy indemnifies a driver for 'legal liability', and as a wife cannot sue her husband for damages there is no legal liability. This unfortunate position can be overcome by extending the policy to cover personal accident benefits or by taking out a separate personal accident policy for the owner's wife.

What is a driver's position if a passenger in his sports car is injured in an accident and the driver's insurance does not cover passenger liability?

If an accident is proved to be the driver's fault he is liable for full compensation out of his own pocket. It is advisable in such circumstances to display a notice in the car which informs passengers that they travel at their own risk, or to make sure passengers know by telling them.

If a used car bought from a dealer shows defects shortly after purchase, has the owner any redress if there has been no written guarantee?

Normally a purchaser must satisfy himself of the condition of the car, but if the state of the car has been said by the dealer to be better than in fact it is, or if defects have been concealed with a view to deceiving a buyer, then the new owner has a case – if he can prove it.

How much must a buyer pay off his hire purchase before a car becomes his own property?

The car does not become the property of the buyer by hire purchase until all the payments have been made. In some hire purchase agreements there is a clause which states: 'If and when all instalments and other moneys payable by the hirer to the owner (usually a finance company) under

What happens if a used car breaks down soon after it is bought?

this agreement have been duly paid, and provided that the hirer shall not have committed any breach of the provisions of this agreement, then the hirer shall have the option (but shall not be bound) to purchase the goods for the sum of ten shillings.' In other words the hirer actually buys the car for a nominal sum after the term of H.P. is finished.

If a car costs less than £300 can a finance company repossess it if payments are delayed?

If the price of a car – or anything else – bought on H.P. is less than £300, or £1,000 in the case of livestock, the hirer is protected by the Hire Purchase Acts which state that goods may not be repossessed without a Court Order. If the hire purchase price is over £300 the Act does not protect the hirer, and if payments fall behind the 'owner' – the finance company – may take the goods away. Cars have been driven away by representatives of a finance company from the roadside in front of a hirer's house – and they have been quite within the law in doing so.

Has a private 'No parking' sign put up in front of a house any legal value?

None at all. The road outside a house is public property and can be used by anyone. However, if cars parked outside a house block a garage entrance the owners can be charged with obstruction. If a large van constantly prevents light reaching a front room, then the owner of the house should consult a solicitor.

Can a car owner sue a garage proprietor for sub-standard repairs even if he has not immediately detected them?

If he discovers them in reasonable time and it is obvious that they were below standard, then he has a case.

Is the Highway Code law?

The Highway Code is not part of the law; it is a standard of conduct suggested by the Ministry of Transport; but breaking the Code may involve a driver in other charges. Incidentally there is no law of the land which states that motorists must drive on the left of the road in Britain – but it would obviously be unwise to flout the Highway Code in this case!

The car owner may be charged with obstruction

What is the definition of obstruction?

Obstruction is the 'unreasonable use of the highway whereby persons or vehicles are (or might be) obstructed.' It is not necessary to prove that road users *are* obstructed, only that they might be obstructed.

What is 'dangerous driving'?

In the Road Traffic Act dangerous driving is described thus: 'If any person drives a motor vehicle on a road recklessly, or at a speed, or in a manner which is dangerous to the public, having regard to all the circumstances of the case, including the nature, condition, and use of the road, and the amount of traffic that is actually at the time or which might reasonably be expected to be, on the road' he is guilty of dangerous driving. The penalties are, on summary conviction (i.e. at a Magistrate's Court) a fine not exceeding £100 or imprisonment for (on the first conviction) not more than four months. On the second conviction the penalty can be six months and a fine of £100. On a conviction on indictment, the penalty can be up to two years' imprisonment and a stiff fine. A driver is

Reckless overtaking may have serious consequences

automatically disqualified if he has three endorsements on his licence within a period of three years.

In all cases the driver's licence will be endorsed. On the first conviction a driver may be disqualified from driving, and on the second conviction he most certainly will be disqualified for a period of not less than nine months, unless his first conviction was more than three years earlier, in which case the Court might see fit not to disqualify.

What are 'special reasons' for not being disqualified?

'Special reasons' relate only to the offence, not to the offender. Therefore a clean driving record, good character, the fact that a licence to drive is needed for the continuance of a business and so on, are not special reasons which may be brought forward in the hope that they will prevent disqualification. The fact that the driver was rushing to a hospital to save a life might well help in such a case.

What is careless driving?

This is an offence that, one might say, is a degree less than dangerous driving. The Act says: 'If any person drives a motor vehicle on a road without due care and attention or without reasonable consideration for other persons using the road he shall be guilty of an offence.' Maximum fine for a first offence is £40; second or subsequent offences can bring a fine of not more than £80 and/or three months' imprisonment. The first conviction could (but does not usually) bring one month's disqualification.

How is driving when under the influence of drink or drugs defined?

A person who when driving or attempting to drive a vehicle on a road is unfit to properly control of the vehicle due to the influence of drink or drugs can be arrested (without a warrant) by a police officer and taken to the station. He can refuse to be examined by the doctor appointed by the Police, by asking for his own to attend.

If a driver who has his car keys in his pocket visits a friend's house and has too much to drink, can he be said to be 'drunk in charge', even though he does not intend driving again that night?

At one time he could. Today, however,

the law states: 'He shall be deemed ... not to have been in charge of a motor vehicle if he proves that at the material time the circumstances were such that there was no likelihood of his driving the vehicle so long as he remained unfit to drive through drink or drugs, and that between becoming unfit to drive and the material time he had not driven the vehicle.' Basically if a person locks his car away in his garage, goes indoors and has a party, he cannot be 'drunk in charge.' If, however, the car is left on the road in front of a friend's house while he visits a drinking party he may possibly be charged with the offence, if it can be proved that he would be driving home again the same evening.

How long does an endorsement remain on a driving licence?

An application for a new (clean) licence may be made to the local council after one year, providing there has been no other offence during that year. In the case of dangerous or careless driving the time limit is three years, providing there has been no similar offence.

Is racing on a public road an offence even though it might be outside the speed limit and in a rural area?

Not only is racing itself an offence, but anyone who promotes a race or a trial of speed on a public highway may be charged with an offence. It can mean imprisonment and a fine.

Can one leave a stationary car in gear on the side of a road, instead of applying the handbrake?

Legally, no. A vehicle that is left unattended by a driver on a public road must have its handbrake set and its engine stopped.

What are the driving offences that can bring disqualification?

Driving under 'the influence' will usually bring automatic disqualification, as will a conviction for being found drunk in charge of a vehicle. A driver will also be disqualified for promoting or taking part in a motor race or speed trial on the highway.

Disqualification may also be ordered on a second or subsequent conviction for dangerous or reckless driving, unless three or more years have elapsed since the previous conviction, or there is some other special reason (connected with the offence). It may be imposed for speeding, and for driving and taking away a vehicle without the owner's consent, or for using an uninsured vehicle. It can be ordered for the seemingly small offence of failing to conform to a traffic sign.

How soon must warning of prosecution be given after an offence?

In cases of speeding, dangerous or careless driving, notice of prosecution must be given within fourteen days unless the driver was warned at the time he might be prosecuted. There are exceptions: if the Police have to spend some time in tracing an owner – he may not have stopped at the time of the offence – the fourteen days rule does not apply. For parking and other such offences the time limit is longer.

Must a motorist attend court when summoned to do so?

Not necessarily for a minor offence: he can plead 'Guilty' by post. For more serious offences he must appear personally. The summons will make this quite clear. A motorist cannot plead 'Not Guilty' by post.

Can a motorist fit a bell or siren to his car?

No; these forms of warning can be used only by hospital services, the Fire Brigade or the Police. Even a cyclist must not fit a siren, although, of course, he may use a bell.

When can a car be parked without lights on a road at night?

In London, one is permitted to park (on the correct side) without lights on a speed limited road that is not a bus route. One must park at least 15 yards away from a junction and within 25 yards of a street lamp which is kept alight all night. In some parts of Britain a night parking notice – a black band on a white square – is put up for the purpose of permitting parking without lights, but motorists who use the area must also comply with the restrictions mentioned above.

Can one policeman successfully charge a motorist with speeding by observation from the roadside?

Normally the evidence of one person who is of the opinion that the motorist was speeding is not enough. One policeman may use a stop-watch to judge the time taken between two points, just as one policeman in a car may give as evidence the reading of his own speedometer. In other words evidence must be fact, not opinion, although if the motorist were travelling really fast the Court may prefer the opinion of the police officer to that of the motorist!

What help will the motoring organisations give the motorist who is charged with an offence?

Both the A.A. and the R.A.C. provide members with free legal representation at Magistrates' Courts except in certain criminal cases or those involving drink. They will on occasion extend this service to manslaughter charges under their free scheme. They both give free legal advice to their members on all subjects connected with motoring and motor cars.

How long should a driver have been fully qualified to drive in order to teach a learner?

It may sound odd, but a driver can teach a learner immediately on passing his test.

Is the vehicle 'Five Year Test' compulsory?

Yes, and cars of five years old or more must be rechecked and a new certificate issued every year.

Are the rules on motorways different from those on ordinary roads?

Yes, in several ways. Firstly, pedestrians, learners, bicycles and motor cycles under 50 c.c. capacity, and certain very large vehicles, are not allowed on a motorway. Reversing, or turning in the carriageway or crossing the central section, is prohibited. Stopping on the carriageway (unless unavoidable) and on the verge (except in emergency) is also forbidden, so do not take your picnic to the M1 and expect to eat it in peace!

Do all vehicles carry purchase tax?

No, only private vehicles are subject to

purchase tax. Many people today buy small vans, which are exempt from the tax, as private transport. For instance a Ford Anglia costs £585, but its commercial counterpart, the 5-cwt Ford van, costs only £379.

May windows be cut into the side of a van?

They may, but the van is then subject to purchase tax. If one owner has kept a van for a minimum of four years, then side windows may be inserted without payment of purchase tax. The road tax is the same in all cases.

May a commercial vehicle be used freely for private purposes?

Yes, there are no restrictions on use, and one may also construct seats in the back of the van for passengers.

If a driver can prove that he has posted his application and money for a new vehicle licence, may he use his car?

No. This point was settled recently at a Magistrates' Court. A motorist proved beyond doubt that he had sent in his application but was convicted for not having a licence on display in the correct position.

May a person sit on the roof of a car whilst it is moving?

He could have sat there before 1962, but now a new regulation forbids it.

If delivery of a car is promised by a dealer on a certain day may a prospective customer refuse to accept it if it is late?

This would be a dangerous move: the delivery promise must be proved. A company was awarded £75 loss of profit in a case of this type when they denied promising delivery on the date claimed by the client, even though they admitted that the car could have been sold to someone else within a week.

Must a car stop if pedestrians are waiting to cross a zebra crossing?

Only if they are actually on the crossing. The fact that a pedestrian is standing on the pavement does not oblige a driver to halt. But as all drivers know, it is as well to keep a weather eye open for teetering pedestrians.

If a pedestrian runs suddenly and carelessly across a zebra, and a driver, who may be taking great care, hits him, who is at fault?

Unfortunately the driver will be blamed. No matter what foolishness the pedestrian may indulge in, if he is on the crossing he is entitled to free passage, and if he is hit by the most careful driver, who may have been unable to avoid him, the driver will still be in the wrong.

If a continuous crowd is using a zebra crossing how does a motorist ever start moving again?

There appears to be no regulation covering this contingency. It happens quite frequently in crowded places and at rush hours, and causes great disruption of traffic. The motorist just has to wait until he sees a gap.

Can a motorist take action against a pedestrian who is dawdling across a zebra crossing?

Yes, if the pedestrian is really slow. The

regulations state that no pedestrian shall remain on the carriageway longer than is necessary to cross. If he does, he can be fined £10.

Is it compulsory to obey a signal to stop given by a School Crossing Patrol?

Yes, when the signal is given by a Ministry of Transport sign, which in fact is always used.

If a private road sign reads 'Danger: Concealed Turning' near the drive to a large house does it make any difference at law if a passing car collides with another car coming from the house?

No, such a sign would have no legal force, and the Court would come to the same decision as if there were no sign.

Are there any rules governing the hours a driver may drive a commercial or public service vehicle?

Yes, a law that protects drivers and public alike states that drivers in these categories may not drive:

1. For more that $5\frac{1}{2}$ hours without a break, or

2. For more than 11 hours in any period of 24 hours commencing two hours after midnight, or

3. So that they have at least 10 consecutive hours for rest in 24 hours calculated from the commencement of any period of driving.

May a cyclist be prosecuted for dangerous riding?

Yes; if a cyclist is proved to be riding in a reckless or dangerous way he may be fined up to £30 or imprisoned for up to 3 months. Inconsiderate cycling is also punishable by a fine.

Does the law state that a cyclist must not ride under the influence of drink?

Yes, and the fine for the first offence is up to £30.

Is a cycle race on the public highway banned by law?

Yes, unless it is authorised by the local authorities.

A cyclist rides straight into trouble

May a cyclist give someone a lift on his bicycle?

No, unless it is constructed or adapted for the purpose.

Must a bicycle have its lights on if it is parked by the side of the road during the hours of darkness?

No, a cyclist need show no lights if he is pushing his cycle, or if it is parked on the left-hand side of the road. If it is parked on the right – just turn it round!

Is it compulsory for a cycle to have a reflector as well as a rear light?

Yes, the law now says that all cycles must carry one – and that they must keep it clean.

What action do the Police take after an accident?

If the accident is of the type in which the Police are interested, and they are convinced that someone is to blame, they will prosecute. They may prosecute one or more people, depending on whether they think that more than one person was at fault. Driving offences fall into three broad categories:

> *(a)* Causing death by reckless or dangerous driving.
> *(b)* Reckless and dangerous driving.
> *(c)* Careless and inconsiderate driving.

If a motorist kills another person he is liable to five years in prison – and disqualification from driving. It must be remembered that charges of dangerous or careless driving may be brought by the Police without the motorist being involved in an accident.

What are the basic regulations with which a vehicle must comply before an owner may drive it on a public road?

The law states that a car must have:

1. A windscreen wiper in working order.
2. A clean windscreen.
3. A mirror (or mirrors) positioned so that traffic behind the car can be seen.
4. A speedometer in working order.
5. A horn in working order.
6. A current road fund licence.
7. Tyres, brakes and steering in good order.

8. Readable number plates.
9. Two side lights and headlight that conform to antidazzle requirements for night driving.
10. Two red rear lights and two reflectors, also for night driving. (The lights must be in working order during the daylight as well as at night.)

A car must not make too much noise and must not emit fumes and smoke.

What type of examination will a car be subjected to on its five-year test?

To pass the test the car must satisfy the following conditions. The owner must ensure that:

Brakes

Brake rods or cables are in good condition, working freely, and do not rub or chafe on other parts.

Bolts and clevis pins are not excessively worn and are secured by split-pins or nuts.

Hydraulic systems are free from visible leaks, and as far as can be judged by the feel on application on the pedal are free from air and properly adjusted.

A 'banger' takes its five-year test

Handbrake pawls and ratchets are not excessively worn, and hold the lever securely in the 'on' position.

Footbrake pedals and hand levers have a reasonable amount of reserve travel when fully applied.

There is no visible evidence of oil leakage round the brake drums or hubs which might indicate that the linings have become affected.

There is no other visible or evident defect in any part of the braking system likely to affect its efficiency.

There is no lack of balance between one wheel and another to cause or to be likely to cause serious pulling to one side. Main brakes on four-wheeled vehicles must be 40 per cent efficient, and secondary brakes 25 per cent. Main brakes operating on two wheels must be at least 30 per cent efficient.

Steering

Track rod, steering arm, and drag link joints are not excessively worn; all securing nuts and split pins are in position. Steering box securely attached.

No excessive wear in king pins or

brushes, no excessive rock in front wheel hub bearings, no excessive play or slackness or restriction of movement in the system as indicated by free movement at the steering wheel.

No other visible or evident defect in any part of the steering mechanism likely to affect its efficiency.

Lighting

Headlamps, spotlamps, etc., over 7 watts are permanently deflected downwards so that, with the vehicle on level ground, a person who is more than 25 feet away and whose eye-level is not less than 3 ft. 6 in. from the ground, will not be dazzled, *or* vehicle fitted with dipping mechanism to prevent dazzle. Obligatory side lights, rear lights, and reflectors are in working order, of the number required by law, and of the size and in position required by law.

CHAPTER SEVEN

HOUSE PURCHASE

What form does a house-purchase contract take?

A contract is a document embodying an agreement between the vendor (seller) and the purchaser, which describes the property and the proposed transaction. It will state whether the property is leasehold or freehold. It will contain conditions governing the deposit to be paid, and will also state in what capacity the vendor is selling the property – whether he is a trustee or the actual owner. It will state what sort of property is offered to the purchaser and whether vacant possession will be given on completion of the transaction. It will, of course, also state the purchase price. These are the basic contents of a contract for the sale or purchase of land (or buildings).

What is the definition of freehold?

The owner of freehold land owns it absolutely and he (or his heirs) own it for ever.

What is leasehold?

Leasehold land is owned by a purchaser for a limited number of years. It may be for ninety-nine years – or it may be as long as nine hundred and ninety-nine. It is rather like a very long rental, and at the end of the term the land and anything on it belongs once more to the original owner. A yearly ground rent must be paid for leasehold property, apart from the agreed price.

That land on which flats are built is usually leased, giving the owners a continuing interest in it and enabling them to lay down certain rules of conduct for the tenants – rules that they would be unable to enforce if the land had been sold freehold.

What does the term 'subject to contract' mean?

When a buyer makes a preliminary agreement to buy a property, and pays a deposit, he often does not wish to be irrevocably bound by the agreement, particularly if it is his intention to instruct a solicitor. Written into the document, which may be no more than a letter, should be the phrase 'subject to contract', which allows the buyer to withdraw from the proposed transaction without losing his deposit, should the building be found to be

Inspecting the house of their dreams

unsuitable (his surveyor may discover that it is unsound or his solicitor may discover some legal defects), or if he changes his mind for any reason. The contents of the final contract itself may also possibly be unfavourable to the buyer and he protects himself by agreeing to buy 'subject to contract'. All reputable estate agents will accept a deposit under these terms.

The prospective buyer undoubtedly has a moral obligation to buy the property if he finds nothing wrong with it or the contract, but if he wishes he can withdraw at any time and buy another house, just as the seller can sell to another person who may have offered a higher price for the house.

What is the usual deposit on a house?

It is usually ten per cent of the purchase price. Many people are confused about the amount of a deposit; some imagine it to be the difference between the price of the house and the amount of money the Building Society will lend them, but that figure bears no relation to the amount that an agent will usually ask the buyer to deposit as a sign of good faith.

What is a mortgage?

A mortgage is a deed by which one can borrow a sum of money, using as security the value – or part of the value – of the house, on the understanding that the house (flat, etc.) becomes the borrower's property once the debt has been finally paid. The term used for the borrower of the money is a mortgagor, and the lender is the mortgagee.

How can one obtain a mortgage?

It can be done in one of the following ways. By application to:

1. A building society.
2. The local council.
3. An insurance company.
4. A bank.
5. Your employer.

The agent through whom the house is bought will know of the various sources of mortgages available and will be able to advise a prospective buyer.

The amount of money that will be lent on a property varies. Usually building societies will advance to owner occupiers only up to 80 per cent of their valuation

Arranging a mortgage with the bank manager

of the house, but on older houses they may only be prepared to lend considerably less.

Is there any difference between a loan from a building society and one from a local council?

Most local councils will advance a loan on mortgage in their own area only. They will often lend two-thirds of their estimate of the value of a house that is not new, and occasionally they will advance the whole of the purchase price on new houses. It depends very much on the council, the housing situation in their district, the state of their treasury, and the financial policy of the country at the time.

Local councils are usually very fair in their dealings with would-be mortgagors – they have no commercial axe to grind as they are non-profit organisations whose business is the welfare of the people. But you will get short shrift from them if you try to raise a large mortgage on a £20,000 house for your wife and two children!

Is there a system of combining a mortgage with life assurance?

Yes. A 'standing' mortgage is obtained,

one on which the interest is repaid, leaving the capital sum as a standing debt. An endowment life policy is taken out at the same time and the premium paid at regular intervals. The life policy – for the same sum as the mortgage – is so arranged that it matures at the same time as the full repayment of the mortgage is due, and it is paid to the mortgagee immediately on maturity.

The main advantage of this system is that if the mortgagor dies at any time before the mortgage is paid, the policy money becomes payable – and the mortgage is thus automatically paid off. This method costs a little more than the straightforward mortgage, but when the saving in income tax is taken into consideration it is very little indeed.

Can a married woman obtain a mortgage?

Anyone who is capable of owning land (house, etc.) is capable of creating a mortgage on it. Usually the lender of the money would require a male to stand as guarantor for such a mortgage, as a woman is not considered to be the breadwinner of the family. A wealthy woman is, of course, viewed more favourably by building societies.

A widow, young and in good permanent employment, may get a mortgage without a great deal of difficulty. There is, however, sometimes some reluctance on the part of lenders to deal with women because of the possibility of childbirth interrupting their ability to earn.

A single woman may also obtain a mortgage providing it can be repaid before retiring age, and that the repayments are less than a quarter of her income.

Can money be borrowed on that part of the mortgage that has been repaid?

Yes, in certain circumstances one can obtain what is called a 'remortgage', but building societies and councils will not usually relend money to buy a car or to repay debts and so on, because their principal function is to lend money to enable a person to purchase a dwelling.

Can a house-owner sell his house and land before the mortgage is completely paid off?

Yes, and most people do this, as not

many owners live in the same house for
the twenty or thirty years term of a mortgage repayment. Out of the proceeds of the
sale, they must first pay off the mortgage –
the mortgage company will have a solicitor
present to receive that part of the money
and to hand over the deeds of the property
which they will have kept in their possession as security. It is not possible to sell your
mortgaged house, keep the whole of the
proceeds and go away to live in a rented
flat!

**What is meant by the term 'second mort-
gage'?**

A second mortgage can sometimes be
obtained when there is already a first mortgage in existence. Perhaps an owner has
paid off a considerable part of his mortgage
on his house, and wishes to raise money for
repairs to the house which the mortgagee
is unwilling to lend. He may then obtain
a second mortgage for the value (or part of
the value) of the money he has already paid
off, or for the 'equity', the balance of the
purchase price which he paid in cash. He
may raise this second mortgage from an

entirely different source than that from which he obtained the first mortgage. If the owner then sells his house, and the first mortgagee has first claim to the part of the money not yet paid to him, then the second mortgagee will take his portion, and the balance will belong to the owner.

The term 'second mortgage' is occasionally confused with what are simply two first mortgages. If the owner wishes to move house, buying another but retaining the first, he would raise another mortgage on his second house. This is just another first mortgage, not a 'second mortgage', which is a special legal term.

In what circumstances has the mortgagee the right to repossess?

The mortgage created by the borrower to the lender will have in it clauses governing the rights of the lender to repossess in the event of a breach of any of the stipulations in the mortgage, such as the failure to pay the mortgage repayments on the due date, or the bankruptcy of the borrower. The lender would then be able to sell the house, or to make such other arrangements as he is entitled to make by law. No building society likes this sort of situation. Although they are generally entitled to begin proceedings if a payment is twenty-eight days in arrears, most lenders would hesitate to exercise their rights until some six months had elapsed.

Is there a limit to the number of mortgaged properties a person may own?

One can have as many as one likes without the approval – or even the knowledge – of the first and subsequent mortgagee. Usually a building society does not ask a client if he has any other mortgages; they may, however, ask about 'other commitments', relying upon the honesty of the client.

Has a mortgagee the right to enter premises?

The mortgage deed will usually stipulate that the mortgagee may enter premises in order to make sure that they are kept in proper repair: usually twice in any one year. In fact, a society rarely inspects a property; the clause is just a safeguard in case the premises are allowed to fall into serious disrepair; they could then put the repairs in hand themselves, and charge the owner for them.

What happens to leasehold property when the lease expires?

A buyer may have purchased a house for a limited number of years – perhaps for the final fifteen of a ninety-nine year period; at the end of that period the land and the property on it reverts to the lessor, the person who originally created the lease, or his successors. The lessee has no rights to the property after that date. Just before the period of the lease ends the lessor would usually send a surveyor to inspect the property, make a schedule of dilapidations, present it to the occupier and demand that the property be brought up to the standard specified in the lease agreement.

What is a title, and how is it investigated?

The title of a property is the chain of ownership, a chain proved by the current owner by the showing of the deeds. In the case of unregistered land, the title which a solicitor is normally required to 'investigate' or check, is thirty years. The title is investigated to make sure that each sale over the years was properly drawn up and that the land legally and rightfully belongs to its present owner.

Unregistered land is land the title to which has not been registered at the Land Registry, possibly because it is not in an area of compulsory registration, or because it has not changed owners since compulsory registration was started in that area.

What is land registration?

It is the formal record at the Land Registry (established by Acts of Parliament) of the land, its description, its owners, agreements affecting it, mortgages upon it, and so on.

The registration of a title under these Acts enables land, houses, etc., to be conveyed (sold) in documents of a much more simple nature than those necessary for unregistered land, saving time and money. It also enables a short document (called a land certificate) to replace bulky deeds; and the validity of the title of the registered owner is guaranteed by the State.

What is an abstract of title?

It is a brief summary of all the title deeds back to a specified date. If a contract states that a 30-year title shall be deduced (produced) an abstract will show a shortened form of all the deeds going back thirty years. It is later checked against the deeds themselves, for a flaw in the legal proceedings of the sale of the land many years ago could, on occasion, cause trouble in the future.

What are the usual costs of buying a house apart from the purchase price?

The charges that a solicitor makes when acting for a buyer are fixed under an Act of Parliament and are based on the sale price, although a solicitor who knows that he will be acting for a client in a complicated purchase may elect to charge such fees that he considers reasonable, and not under the fixed scale.

In the table below the various fees and charges are set out beside the purchase price.

| | SOLICITORS' FEES | | Building Society Charges on Mortgage |
Purchase Price	Unregistered Property	Registered Property	
	£ s	£ s d	£ s
2,000	37 10	25 — —	12 10
3,000	52 10	35 — —	17 10
4,000	60 —	40 — —	22 10
4,500	63 15	41 17 6	26 10
5,000	67 10	43 15 —	27 10

No stamp duty is payable on houses that cost less than £4,500. Over £4,500 the duty is 10s od per £100 on the purchase price, up to £6,000; and over £6,000 the stamp duty is £2 per £100.

There is also an additional stamp duty which must be paid on a newly granted lease of property, a duty that depends on the ground rent and the length of the lease.

STAMP DUTY		LAND REGISTRY FEES	
on Purchase Deed	on Mortgage	First Registration	Subsequent Registration
£	£ s	£ s	£ s
—	5 —	5 —	5 —
—	7 10	7 —	7 10
—	10 —	8 —	10 —
—	11 5	8 10	11 5
25	12 10	9 —	12 10

Is the buyer of a property liable for hidden defects as soon as he has bought it?

Yes, unless he can prove that the defects were deliberately concealed by the seller, and this is not an easy thing to prove. This is why it is important that a purchaser should employ a competent surveyor to inspect the house thoroughly before any binding contract is signed.

With new property the purchaser should

insist on a guarantee in the agreement, or in a separate agreement, that the builder will make good any defects due to faulty materials or bad workmanship that appear in the first six months (or even longer) of occupation, providing they are reported in writing within the time limit.

What are rates?

They are a form of tax levied by the local council on all houses or flats and any other building owners. Rates are used by the council to pay for the local services and amenities such as police, schools, libraries, highway, refuse collection and so on. Each owner pays rates at so much per pound on the rateable value of his property.

How are rates assessed?

They are based on the rateable value of the property, which varies according to the building's size, the area in which it stands, its condition, etc. As from April 1st, 1963 the rateable value is based on the yearly rent which an owner is presumed to be able to obtain for his property today. Business premises are also assessed on their

206

present-day rental values. Agricultural properties are exempt from rates, and so are empty buildings.

How does one object to a valuation?

If the valuation officer has, in the opinion of the householder, assessed the rateable value of the property too highly, he can object when the new figure is presented. The owner may consider that the value is based on a rent that would be impossible to obtain today, or he may find that other similar property in the same area is assessed at less than his own house, or that his house lacks some usual amenity – e.g. it is next door to a noisy factory. If a householder has a sound argument he should certainly object – nothing will be lost, and if he is successful, other charges, like that of water rates, will also be reduced. In fact, the notice of proposal to alter the valuation which is sent out by the local authorities actually invites the owner to object within twenty-eight days.

Can one appeal if an objection fails?

If the valuation officer and the local

rating authority both disagree with the householder's arguments, then he can appeal to the local valuation court. There are no costs to be paid for such an appeal. A last appeal may be made to the Lands Tribunal, but this will involve costs.

What is compulsory purchase?

A compulsory purchase order is normally made by a local authority if it wishes to acquire property in an area for re-development. It is made either for the demolition of unfit houses and the building of blocks of flats to rehouse the occupiers, or for the clearing of buildings in the area in order to construct new roads or similar projects. There can be no appeal against the order itself, but a householder may appeal to the Lands Tribunal against the price offered to him by the council.

The council will first serve a notice to the people affected detailing the proposed scheme and asking for any objections. These will later be heard at a public inquiry before the order for compulsory purchase is made. These meetings are presided over by an inspector of the Ministry of Housing and Local Government, who will advise the Ministry whether the order should be confirmed or rejected by them. If the scheme is confirmed by the Ministry, the local council then serves a 'notice to treat' on the house owner, asking for details of ownership and the price he thinks he should receive for it. The council then enters into negotiations with the owners concerned until a satisfactory price is arranged.

What guarantee has a buyer that his property will not, in a short time, be bought under a compulsory purchase order?

None, although most local authorities have plans made for five or ten years into the future which may be examined by a prospective buyer. However, there is no law that prevents a local planning authority from suddenly changing its mind and deciding to run a new highway through newly bought property. An owner's only safeguard is in an Act of Parliament which states that he must be offered the market value of his property. There have been many legal battles over the estimate of this value.

Searching for the right flat

Set out below is a typical example of a fair and sound agreement for the sale of a newly-built leasehold flat, a type of agreement that is in constant use now that more people buy flats on a 99-year lease, rather than pay a high rent.

THIS AGREEMENT is made the Twenty-Sixth day of January One thousand nine hundred and sixty-three BETWEEN BETTER FLATS LTD whose registered office is at 3 Old Street London W.2 by N. Fison a duly authorised Director (hereinafter called 'the Vendor') of the one part and JOHN GORDON ROGERS of 25 Ridgeway Road Hampstead London N.W.3 (hereinafter called 'the Purchaser') of the other part.

WHEREBY IT IS AGREED as follows:

1. THE Vendor shall grant and the Purchaser shall take a lease of ALL THAT Flat known as Flat 15 Number 5 Hilary Road Harrow Middlesex now or intended to be constructed on the Vendor's Estate fronting Hilary Road Harrow Middlesex TOGETHER with the Garage shown and numbered 30 and the —— Store Area shown and Numbered 15 on the Vendor's said Estate Plan for

the term of NINETY-NINE YEARS from the 25th day of December One thousand nine hundred and sixty-two at the yearly rent of THIRTY POUNDS

2. SUCH Lease shall be in the form of the draft Lease annexed hereto.

3. (i) The Vendor will construct the said premises (hereinafter referred to as 'the demised premises') in a sound and workmanlike manner in accordance with the plans and specifications prepared by the Vendor and which the Purchaser has had the opportunity to inspect and of which (whether he has inspected the same or not) he shall be deemed to have full knowledge and also in accordance with the planning requirements and the by-laws of the local authorities.

(ii) Unless prevented from so doing by strikes lock-outs shortages of material weather wars or other causes not within its control the Vendor will complete the said works not later than the lst day of June One thousand nine hundred and sixty-three or if so prevented so soon thereafter as may be reasonably practicable and the Vendor shall have the right to substitute materials as nearly as may be of the same value in lieu of those contained in the said specification if in its absolute discretion it is deemed expedient so to do and to vary the forms of construction arising from the use of such substituted materials.

4. THE purchase price shall be FOUR THOUSAND THREE HUNDRED AND FIFTY POUNDS of which the sum of FOUR HUNDRED AND THIRTY-FIVE POUNDS as a deposit and in part payment has been paid on the signing hereof to the Vendor and the balance shall be paid as hereinafter provided

5. (i) This Agreement shall be deemed to incorporate the National Conditions of Sale (Sixteenth Edition) so far as the same are not inconsistent with the terms hereof and are applicable to a Sale by private treaty.

(ii) Clause 16 (3) of the said National Conditions shall not apply hereto.

(iii) The demised premises are sold subject to all Local Land Charges whether registered before or after the date hereof and to all matters capable of registration as Local Land Charges whether or not actually so registered.

(iv) The Vendor has obtained the necessary by-law consent and planning permission for the erection of the demised premises as aforesaid. The Vendor will supply copies thereof and the originals thereof may be inspected at the office of the Vendor's Legal Department 16 Westham Road Ilford Essex at any time during office hours prior to completion.

6. THE Vendor's freehold title is registered at Her Majesty's Land Registry with an Absolute Title under Title No. Z 6742 and the abstract shall consist of a copy of the entries in the Register and of any document therein referred to and the filed plan together with an authority to inspect the same.

7. THE demised premises are sold subject to all exceptions reservations covenants

conditions and restrictions entered on the Register affecting the same a copy whereof has been handed to the Purchaser or his solicitor prior to the signing hereof.

8. (i) The purchase shall be completed at 16 Westham Road Ilford aforesaid within fourteen days after written notice of the completion of the said works.

(ii) If any defect shall be discovered in the demised premises before the expiration of six months after completion and the Purchaser shall notify the Vendor thereof in writing before the expiration of such period and such defect shall be directly attributable to defective materials or bad workmanship then the Vendor shall make good such defects without expense to the Purchaser. Save as aforesaid and subject to the terms of the Agreement referred to in sub-clause (iii) hereof the Vendor shall not be under any liability to the Purchaser for any loss or damage arising directly or indirectly out of any defect in the demised premises whether discovered before or after the expiration of the said period or for any defect due to accident misuse neglect natural shrinkage drying out or fair wear and tear and the provisions of this clause shall operate and have effect to the exclusion of any warranty or agreement on the part of the Vendor which would or might be otherwise implied in this Agreement by law.

(iii) The Vendor will deliver to the Purchaser or his solicitor as soon as possible after completion of the said dwellinghouse a Certificate of Compliance with the specification issued by the National House Builders' Registration Council together with the form of Agreement laid down by the said Council and the Purchaser shall deliver to the Vendor a duly signed Counterpart of such Agreement.

(iv) IF any dispute should arise between the parties hereto regarding the nature and extent of the liability of the Vendor to remedy defects due to non-compliance with the specification or as to the date of the completion of each stage or otherwise under this Agreement such dispute shall be referred to the said Registration Council who may nominate a person or persons to consider the facts and whose arbitration and final decision shall be binding upon both parties hereto.

(v) If from any cause whatever (other than the neglect or default of the Vendor) any part of the purchase price is not paid on the date herein before fixed for its payment the Purchaser shall pay interest thereon at the rate of Six pounds per centum per annum until payment.

(vi) If after the date hereof there shall be any increase or decrease in the cost at the date hereof of labour or materials employed or utilised in connection with the erection of the demised premises the purchase price shall be increased or decreased by an equivalent amount and this Agreement shall be read and construed as if such increased or decreased purchase price were substituted for the purchase price mentioned in Clause 4 hereof. In the event of the Vendor claiming that there has been any such increase or decrease the same shall be certified in writing by the Vendor's architect PROVIDED ALWAYS that the said purchase price shall not be increased under this clause by more than Five per cent.

9. UNTIL payment to the Vendor of the balance of all moneys payable to the Vendor hereunder the Purchaser shall not be entitled to take vacant possession of the demised premises.

10. (i) So long after the date hereof as any part of the purchase money or interest thereon shall remain unpaid the Vendor will keep the demised premises (or such part or parts thereof as may have been erected from time to time) insured in the full value thereof against destruction or damage by fire storm tempest and civil aircraft in an

office to be selected by the Vendor and will punctually pay all premiums and other moneys necessary for effecting and keeping on foot such insurance.

(ii) All moneys (if any) received under any such Policy or Policies by the Vendor shall be applied by the Vendor in rebuilding or reinstating the demised premises and the balance (if any) of such moneys shall belong to the Purchaser.

(iii) If at any time the Purchaser is entitled to the benefit of any insurance on the demised premises which is not effected or maintained by the Vendor under the provisions of this clause then all moneys received by virtue of such insurance shall if the Vendor so requires be applied in making good the loss or damage in respect of which the same shall have been received.

11. Until all moneys payable hereunder to the Vendor have been duly paid the Purchaser will not enter into any lease or tenancy agreement of the whole or any part of the demised premises.

12. ALL the terms of the agreement between the parties hereto shall be deemed to be incorporated herein and any statement whether made verbally or contained in any printed advertising or other matter issued by the Vendor or by its agents or on its behalf shall not be deemed to be a term or condition of this Agreement nor to amount to a representation or warranty inducing the same.

AS WITNESS the hands of the parties hereto

SIGNED by the said N. Fison }
on behalf of the Vendor

  for and on behalf of
    BETTER FLATS LIMITED

SIGNED by the Purchaser }

(NOTE. — It is not possible in a work of this nature to print the form of the lease, which is a rather lengthy document.)

LANDLORD AND TENANT

CHAPTER EIGHT

LANDLORD
AND
TENANT

What type of rented accommodation is still let at a controlled rent?

All unfurnished rented houses, flats and other accommodation that had on November 7th, 1956, a rateable value of £40 and under in London, and £30 and under in other parts of England and Wales. But all tenancies that began later than July 5th, 1957 are free from control, whatever the rateable value of the accommodation.

How permanent is the security of tenure (protection against eviction) of a tenant occupying a rent controlled house?

The tenant is secure, all other things considered, for as long as the Act is in force. But this does not mean that all people in rent-controlled accommodation can look forward to a lifetime of security, for the Act may be amended by Parliament at any time if circumstances in the country make it necessary or advisable.

May a landlord serve notice on a tenant who has lived in a controlled house for ten years?

He may serve it, but the tenant could

ignore it, except in certain circumstances which permit the landlord to repossess his house. These are:

1. Where the tenant is in arrears with his rent or otherwise in breach of the conditions of his tenancy.
2. Where a tenant or lodger has caused a nuisance or annoyance to adjoining occupiers or has permitted the condition of the house to run down.
3. When a tenant has given notice that he is quitting the house, and the landlord had contracted to sell the house.
4. When the tenant has without the landlord's permission assigned or sublet the whole of the premises.
5. Where the house is so overcrowded that it contravenes the Housing Act of 1957.
6. When the tenant was employed by the landlord who now needs it to accommodate another employee.
7. When the house is required by the landlord (provided that he bought the house before November 7th, 1956) for his own accommodation, or that of his son or daughter over 18 years of age, or for his mother or father. In this case the

Court must decide whether taking alternative accommodation would be more of a hardship for the landlord or the tenant.

8. When the Court is satisfied that suitable alternative accommodation has been made available by the landlord for the tenant.

No Court will make an order for possession unless it is convinced that no undue hardship is caused to the tenant, regardless of the points set out above. It would be wise for a tenant to take legal advice if any of these points arise.

What is 'suitable alternative accommodation'?

This again is a matter for the Court to decide. It should not be further away from a tenant's place of work than the original accommodation or more difficult to travel to. It would have to contain a similar number of rooms of about the same size, and it would have to be at approximately the same rent. Whilst the type of district in which the alternative accommodation is situated is not usually a relevant point, the character of the house itself may be. The accommodation must be available at the date of the hearing of the court case and at the date when the Court orders the tenant to vacate.

If a landlord sells a rent-controlled house in which a tenant lives may the new owner serve notice to quit because he wishes to live in it himself?

If he did, it would not be enforceable. As he had not bought the house before November 7th, 1956 he would have no right to possession on grounds of wanting it for himself or his family. Of course, he has the usual rights if a tenant does not pay his rent, etc. Houses are often sold with 'part possession', when perhaps the upper flat is occupied by a tenant who is protected under the Act, and the lower flat is empty.

If a tenant of a rent-controlled house dies, is his family liable to be given notice to leave?

If a statutory tenant (one that occupies a house or flat which has a controlled rent) dies, the tenancy passes to his widow, or to any member of his family who has been living at the house as part of his family for at least six months immediately before his death. There has been much argument over who exactly is a member of the family, but it usually means a son, daughter or close relative. The tenancy can be transferred only once in this way. The second tenant is protected in the same way as the original one.

If the rateable value of a house is increased, perhaps because the landlord has added a garage, does it affect rent control?

No, because the Act states that rents are controlled if the rateable value was under the figure previously mentioned, at November 7th, 1956. Any later fluctuation does not affect the circumstances.

If the rates of a rent-restricted flat or house are increased may the landlord increase the rent?

Yes, the landlord may pass on to the tenant the portion of the rates for which his accommodation is liable. If the rates go down the tenant would be entitled to a reduction in rent.

If a tenant who has been living in accommodation since before July 1957 thinks he may be paying more than the maximum rent may he still have it reduced?

If the conditions are within the limits set out in the first paragraph of this chapter he may get it reduced, and he would be entitled to a refund of his overpayment for the last two years.

May the tenant of a rent-controlled house sub-let?

Unless he has agreed with his landlord not to do so, he may sub-let part of his premises but not all of them.

What repairs must the landlord make to a rent-controlled house, and does the extent of the repairs make any difference to the rent?

If the landlord arranged that the tenant does all the repairs to the house he may charge a yearly rent of one and one-third times the gross value of the house plus the rates; if the tenant does the inside repairs only the landlord can charge double the gross value plus rates, and if the landlord elects to do all the repairs himself then he can charge two and one-third times the gross value plus rates. These are the maximum rentals chargeable under the Rent Act.

Are furnished flats rent controlled?

Yes, to a limited extent, if they come under the conditions set out in the first paragraph: i.e. if the ratcable value is less than £40 in London or £30 elsewhere and the tenancy commenced before July 5th, 1957. Security of tenancy may be obtained in two distinct ways: the first as the result of making a reference relating to the rent, and the second as the result of applying for security of tenancy. Unlike the Rent Act, the Furnished House (Rent Control) Act provides security of tenure by rendering notices to quit ineffective, and not by imposing a prohibition upon the making of an order for possession.

What is the definition of a furnished flat?

It is defined as a flat where a substantial

portion of the rent is attributable to the furniture. A table, bedstead and a couple of chairs in a flat would not constitute furnished accommodation, as very little rent could be charged for it.

Should a written agreement be made when a person intends to rent a flat or house?

There need be no written agreement if the tenancy is for less than three years, but it is always wise to have any agreement in writing. For no matter how short a period, a tenancy agreement will keep both parties much happier. It can be prepared by a solicitor for a reasonable fee, or a printed form bought – but never sign any document without first reading and understanding it, or getting a solicitor to explain it to you.

Can a landlord give a week's notice to the tenant of uncontrolled accommodation if the rent is paid weekly?

No, the landlord must give a minimum of one month's notice to a tenant regardless of how frequently the rent is paid, unless there is a clause in their agreement stating that longer notice is required by either side. If the tenant leaves without notice of his intention to quit, the landlord can recover rent for a week, month or quarter beyond the time of the tenant's leaving, according to whether the rent was paid weekly, monthly or quarterly.

How long may rent fall in arrears before the landlord can take action?

He could, in theory, take action a day later, but in practice the Court will always grant maximum relief to a tenant – rather than make an order for possession they will give the tenant every opportunity to bring his rent up to date. Since any hearing on this subject would normally be at the County Court it would in any case be several weeks before the matter came to court.

What action may a landlord take if rent falls in arrears?

He may apply for an order to repossess, or to evict the tenant, or he may ask permission of the Court to send in bailiffs to recover and sell enough of the tenant's goods to pay for the arrears, or he may sue for the amount owing, plus legal costs.

If a flat is taken for two years and the tenant finds that he has to leave the area in six months, may he sub-let the flat?

It depends on the agreement. The usual clause that the landlord puts into an agreement is that the tenant shall not assign, sublet or part with possession of the premises without the consent in writing of the landlord, which shall not be unreasonably refused. Usually the tenant is able to sub-let or assign to a responsible person. On the other hand if the landlord has let the flat for a fixed short term the agreement may prohibit sub-letting altogether. In that case the tenant would have to continue paying until the lease expired.

What is 'assignment'?

If a tenant assigns his lease to another person, he passes on his responsibility and the new tenant pays his rent directly to the landlord. If he sub-lets, he is in effect the new tenant's landlord, and receives the rent from him: his lease remains in his possession and its conditions are his responsibility.

What is 'fair wear and tear'?

Most tenancy and lease agreements state that the tenant is responsible for certain repairs, 'fair wear and tear excepted'. This means that he is not responsible for any deterioration due to normal and reasonable use of the furniture, walls, fixtures, etc. But it does not relieve him of the responsibility for a defect that may have been originally fair wear and tear, but which he has allowed to develop into a serious fault.

If a fire destroys a tenant's house must he rebuild it at his own expense?

If there is no clause in the agreement that the tenant is responsible for repairs or insurance, then no action could be taken by the landlord; similarly if the agreement contains words to the effect that 'tempest or accidental fire' are not the tenant's worry. Otherwise he should insure the building so that he is covered against any loss.

Is a landlord entitled to charge for fixtures and fittings when letting a flat?

Yes; today he may sell to the tenant removable fixtures, and may charge whatever he wishes, regardless of their market value. He may also charge for services such as for cleaning the common parts of the house or block of flats.

Are the tenants of a block of flats responsible for repairs to the roof, stairs, halls, landings, etc.?

Unless the agreement states otherwise the common parts of the flats are the landlord's responsibility, and he must keep them in good repair. If the roof leaks and damages a tenant's flat, the landlord must make good the damage.

The Housing Act, 1961 imposes on landlords of dwelling houses a number of important repairing obligations in the case of weekly and other tenancies, including leases up to seven years (with certain exceptions); and the Act will not recognise an attempt by landlords to pass these obligations on to their tenants. The landlord's obligations include keeping in repair the structure and the exterior of dwelling houses including drains and gutters, and the internal installations for the supply of water, gas and electricity and for sanitation (including basins, sinks, baths and toilets) and for space heating or heating water. These are subject to a number of conditions.

When a tenant leaves his flat or rented house may he take plants and shrubs that he has planted himself?

No, he may not, except by agreement with the landlord. Any growing things become 'part of the soil' and belong to the landlord. The same rule applies to a greenhouse that has proper foundations, or a garage that is fixed to the ground.

May a tenant take his own fixtures with him when he leaves rented accommodation?

Only if he can remove them without damaging the structure of the house. If he installs piped heating or a kitchen range that has involved knocking holes in the wall, he will have to leave them there.

The following is an example of a normal tenancy agreement between a landlord and a tenant: this one is for three years.

AN AGREEMENT made the 10th day of January One thousand nine hundred and sixty-three BETWEEN MARY EVA ADA JONES of 43 Haverford Road, St Albans Herts Spinster (hereinafter called 'the Landlord') of the one part and JOHN ALAN RICHARDS of 14 Willow Drive Marylebone London W.10 (hereinafter called 'the Tenant') of the other part WHEREBY it is agreed as follows:

1. The Landlord agrees to let and the Tenant agrees to take ALL THAT flat or suite of rooms on the first floor of the building known as 14 Willow Drive Marylebone aforesaid (hereinafter called 'the premises') together with the use of the bathroom on the first floor in common with the tenant of the ground floor flat TOGETHER with the right to pass and repass over the path leading

from the street to the front door of said building and over the entrance hall and staircase leading to the premises together with the use of all fixtures and fittings of the Landlord in or upon the premises and the bathroom for the term of Three Years from the 7th day of January One thousand nine hundred and sixty-three at the yearly rent of ONE HUNDRED AND FIFTY-SIX POUNDS (clear of all deduction) payable in advance by equal weekly payments of £3 0s 0d on Saturday of each week during the continuance of this Agreement the first of such payments to be made on the signing hereof.

2. The Tenant agrees with the Landlord as follows:

(1) To pay the said rent on the days and in manner aforesaid.

(2) To keep the premises in a clean and tidy condition.

(3) To be responsible (save as to damage caused by fire or other normally insurable risks) for all internal repairs and decorations to the premises and for the maintenance repair or replacement of all internal fittings in the nature of

tenant's fittings Provided that the Tenant shall not be liable for repairs to the roof of the exterior or the structure or timbers of the building and will at the expiration or sooner determination of the said term deliver up to the Landlord the premises in such good repair order and condition (except as aforesaid).

(4) To permit the Landlord and her agent with or without workmen and others at all reasonable times upon reasonable notice to enter upon the premises to examine the state and condition thereof and to give the tenant notice in writing of all dilapidations and wants of reparation cleansing painting or amendments to the premises then found and by such notice to require the Tenant to repair cleanse paint and amend the premises in accordance with sub-Clause (3) hereof within the month then next following within which time the Tenant hereby agrees to so repair cleanse paint and amend the same accordingly.

(5) To use the premises as and for a single private dwelling house only and not to carry on or permit to be carried on upon the premises or any part thereof

any profession trade or business what-soever.

(6) Not to do or suffer to be done in or upon the premises or any part thereof any act or thing which may be or become a nuisance damage inconvenience or annoyance to the Landlord or the tenants or the occupants of any adjoining premises and to keep all rooms in the premises properly carpeted and not to play or allow to be played any wireless television instrumental or mechanical music between the hours of 11 p.m. and 8 a.m. so as to be a nuisance or annoyance to neighbours.

(7) Not to assign underlet or part with the possession of the premises or any part thereof except with the Landlord's consent first obtained and such consent not to be unreasonably withheld.

(8) Not to do or permit to be done anything on the premises whereby any increased or extra premium may become payable for the insurance of the premises against loss or damage by fire or any policy for such insurance may become void or voidable.

(9) Within seven days after receipt of

any notice or order made or given by any competent authority in respect of the premises to give full particulars thereof to the Landlord to take all reasonable steps to comply with the same and to join with the Landlord in taking such other action in relation thereto as the Landlord shall decide

3. Provided always that if and when the said rent or any part thereof shall be in arrear for fourteen days after the same shall have become due (whether legally demanded or not) or if the Tenant shall commit a breach of any of the several agreements and stipulations herein contained and on his part to be observed and performed or if the Tenant shall become bankrupt or assign his estate or execute any deed of arrangement for the benefit of his creditors then and in such case it shall be lawful for the Landlord to re-enter upon the premises and the same have again repossess and enjoy as in his former estate as if this Agreement had never been made but without prejudice to any claims the Landlord may have thereunder in respect of

any breach of any agreement by the Tenant.

4. The Landlord agrees with the Tenant (*a*) that the Tenant paying the rent hereby reserved and performing and observing all the agreements by the Tenant herein contained may quietly possess and enjoy the premises during the tenancy without any interruption by the Landlord (here meaning only the party hereto personally and not any other reversioner) or any person claiming under or in trust for him and (*b*) to keep the roof exterior structure and common parts of the said building in good repair decoration and condition and insured against all usually insurable risks and to keep the common parts cleaned and lighted during usual hours.

5. In the event of the premises being destroyed by fire so as to be rendered unfit for occupation the rent hereby reserved or a proportionate part thereof according to the nature and extent of the injury sustained shall cease to be payable until the premises shall have

been restored and reinstated and made
fit for occupation:

AS WITNESS the hands of the parties
hereto

SIGNED by the said EVA
ADA JONES in the
presence of:

CHAPTER NINE

PROBLEMS
AT
WORK

What are the legal duties of an employer to his employees?

He must take care not to expose his employees to undue risk, and anyone who is hurt at work should immediately consult his trade union or a solicitor. The employer must also take the responsibility for any trouble arising out of his orders to his employees if they believed that his orders were within the law when they carried them out. He has no duty to provide medical care (except in works and factories), nor is he responsible for trouble arising out of employees' disregard of his orders.

What are the legal duties of employee to employer?

He must, of course, obey any reasonable orders. He must not work for any of his firm's competitors – even in his off-duty hours, and he must not disclose any of his employer's commercial secrets to anyone. An employer can take legal action against an employee who works privately for any of the employer's clients on similar business to that of his company.

If no written contract is made between an employer and his employee is he entitled to leave at a moment's notice?

No. When a person is hired to work for another, a contract of service is implied whether it is in writing or not. If wages are paid weekly it may be assumed that a week's notice is the minimum on either side. If any employee leaves without giving that notice he may be sued for breach of contract, unless he can show good cause for leaving.

May an employer dismiss an employee at a moment's notice?

The employer is bound by the same rules as his employee, although he too may find good cause for dismissal. These are laid down as:

1. Habitual negligence.
2. Conduct calculated to injure the employer's business.
3. Wilful disobedience to lawful orders.
4. Gross moral misconduct.
5. Dishonesty.
6. Drunkenness.
7. Permanent disability from illness and similar reasons.

'You're fired!'

If an employee considers that he has been wrongfully dismissed he may sue for breach of contract, and if he succeeds in the action he may recover damages for lost wages and inconvenience.

If no contract has been made between employer and employee how is the length of notice decided?

In the past there have been many cases on this subject. The only way to find out is by looking up the previous decisions of the Court in a similar case. For instance the Court has stated that reasonable notice for an ordinary commercial traveller was one month, and for a specialist salesman, three months; a journalist was allowed six months, and the chief officer of a ship, one year.

Must an employer give his employee a testimonial when he leaves?

No; there is nothing in the law which forces him to write a testimonial, good or bad.

May an employer sue his employee if the latter damages equipment at work?

Yes, if the damage was caused by the employee's negligence.

Can an employer insist that his employee does not open a similar business or work for a rival firm when he leaves?

He may certainly write it into the contract, and if he does, and the employee signs it, it has legal force if the law considers it reasonable — which it often does not — and it is up to the employee to object before he signs the contract if he disagrees with the condition.

Is an employer responsible for damages (that may have nothing to do with his business) caused by an employee outside his office or factory?

It may seem hard, but the answer is usually, yes. For instance if a solicitor's clerk persuaded a client to sign documents that he described as a mere formality, when in fact they were a transfer of money to himself, his firm would be held responsible. Similarly if an errand boy cyclist injured a pedestrian in the course of making deliveries, his employer would be liable for damages. But if he injured anyone on the way to lunch his employer would not be liable. If an office worker left a tap running in the ladies' cloakroom and overnight it flooded the shop downstairs, her employer could be sued. The rule is: an employer is responsible for the wrongs of his servants if they are committed in the course of their employment. And in the course of their employment employees necessarily do many things that are not directly connected with their work, but the employer is responsible for all of them! He may also be liable for an employee's criminal acts, if the victim has suffered injury or loss.

If a scientific worker makes a discovery or invents something during working hours and in the normal course of his work, to whom does its value belong?

The value of all work done in working hours belongs to the employer.

Is it an offence in law to alter a testimonial before presenting it to a new employer?

Yes, it certainly is, just as forging a testimonial is a criminal offence. If proved, the punishment may be a heavy fine or imprisonment.

May an employer pay wages in goods?

He cannot insist on it; under an old Act the law entitles an employee to be paid in money. Of course, it may be done by mutual agreement – such as the provision of produce for a farm worker.

Must an employer pay wages to an employee who is away sick?

There is no hard and fast rule, and it depends on the contract between them. If no contract was made when the employee joined the company, he will have to find out what is the normal practice and custom in his trade. If it is customary to be paid while sick, then he would have a good claim in law against an employer who refused to pay. An employer is not bound to pay an employee who is away simply because he feels like a day off.

251

What is the Factories Act?

The Factories Act 1961 is the result of years of legislation for the protection of the health, safety and general welfare of factory workers. To ensure that the terms of the Act are carried out the Ministry of Labour has inspectors who regularly visit factories. Amongst its thousands of stipulations, the Factories Act states that each person working in a factory must have 400 cubic feet of space to himself; this could be a floor space of 4 by 7 feet by about 14 feet high – but one must take the unoccupied part of a room into account in the calculation. The Act also states that drinking water and washing facilities must be provided, and that a first aid box must be available.

Must a shop close on 'early closing' day?

The Shop Act says that a shop must close no later than one o'clock on one day every week. Shopkeepers may, within limits, change the day to suit themselves. The local authorities may fix the day for the closing of various types of shops if the majority of owners of that type approve.

Overcrowding in factories is illegal

If early closing day falls on a Bank Holiday, the proprietor may keep his shop open on the early closing day before or after the holiday. There are certain types of shops which are exempt from the early closing rule. They are public houses, restaurants, garages and accessory shops, newspaper shops, perishable food shops, tobacconists, railway bookstalls, and shops which sell medical supplies. But if a chemist's shop is open under this exemption one can buy only medical or surgical goods there.

Can an employer insist that an assistant works in the afternoon of an early closing day, perhaps to stocktake?

No; each assistant must by law finish work at 1.30 p.m. one day a week.

If an assistant works on Sunday morning may he claim another half-day off for it?

Yes. In fact he can claim a complete day if he has been employed for more than four hours on a Sunday. And the day should be one during the following week. Check first, though — there are certain exceptions to this rule.

Peaceful picketing

Are the maximum permitted working hours of a fifteen-year-old restricted?

Yes; the Act states that a person of under 16 must not be employed for more than forty-four hours a week. It also states that people between 16 and 18 must not work for more than forty-eight hours a week. However, if business pressure is great, they may be employed on overtime work, subject to time limits.

Is picketing during strikes legal?

Yes, the law allows what it calls 'peaceful picketing', but not the use of force or threats to stop a person going to work during a strike.

(The foregoing must be read subject to the official schemes and regulations governing the conditions of employment in many specified trades, often conferring substantial benefits on employees in that trade – e.g. specified hours, holidays with pay, etc. Also, Parliament is considering passing an Act which will regulate service agreements between employers and employees, and another Act regulating conditions of work in offices.)

CHAPTER TEN

THE
COURTS

What are Courts of Summary Jurisdiction?

They are Courts that try minor offences, such as cases relating to motoring, drunkenness, cruelty to animals, and so on. They also remit for trial by a higher Court people whose offence merits more punishment than this Court can award – which is usually a maximum of six months. It is empowered to deal with small domestic civil matters and local licensing.

Courts of Summary Jurisdiction are held before lay magistrates who may be Justices of the Peace, men of standing who give their services to the Court without payment and who are not members of the legal profession. J.P.s are appointed by the Crown for their integrity, not their legal knowledge, and although there is often complaint about their capabilities, their very lack of legal training more often than not allows them more understanding and insight into the problems of the defendant.

These Courts may also be held before a Stipendiary Magistrate, who is a paid officer of the Court, or before a salaried Metropolitan Police Magistrate.

A Magistrates' Court has an important

figure called the Clerk of the Court. He is usually a qualified solicitor, who sits below the bench and gives his expert advice to lay magistrates on points of the law.

The Courts of Summary Jurisdiction have a special division called a Juvenile Court. These are set up to deal with the offences of children. They are deliberately held in a very informal manner, with a minimum of legal ceremony. The magistrates usually sit at a table and the child before them is allowed to tell his story in his own way. The public are excluded and the Press is not allowed to publish the names of the defendants. The whole atmosphere of a Juvenile Court is one of friendliness and help, and the object of the Court is to advise rather than punish, although, of course, it must award punishment when it is merited.

What are the Assizes?

These are really a branch of the High Court, and are held in different parts of the country to judge both civil and criminal cases. The Judges go out 'on circuit' and visit various areas three or four times

A magistrates' court in session

a year. The criminal cases that come before this Court are those that have been passed on by the Magistrates' Court for trial.

What is the Central Criminal Court?

Popularly known as the Old Bailey, the Central Criminal Court is held twelve times a year in London. It was set up during the last century to try all major crimes committed in the vicinity of London.

Who is liable for jury service?

As a general rule all householders between the ages of 21 and 60.

What is a County Court?

The County Courts are Civil Courts, presided over by a paid Judge (who must be a barrister of over seven years standing) and assisted by a Registrar. These Courts, which are situated throughout the country, deal with civil actions for damages, debts, disputes involving contracts or rents, and troubles connected with hire purchase. If money in the form of debts or damages is the subject of an action the County Court is usually restricted to dealing with amounts of less than £400.

What are Quarter Sessions?

They have a double role. This Court hears appeals from the Magistrates' Court, when the decision of that Court is questioned, and it tries offences of more gravity than can be dealt with by the Magistrates' Court, with the exception of homicide and other really serious crimes, which are usually tried at the Assizes.

Generally County Quarter Sessions are held before a Chairman, who is a fully qualified barrister of ten years' standing, and the Borough Quarter Sessions are presided over by a Recorder.

What is the work of the High Courts?

The High Court is divided into several divisions: for example, the Probate, Divorce and Admiralty Division deals with divorce, the proving of wills and collisions of ships at sea. The Chancery Division deals with problems involving trusts, partnerships, mortgages, etc. Wards of Court are also the concern of this Division. The Queen's Bench

263

Division, under the presidency of the Lord Chief Justice, hears cases of libel, matters arising out of breach of contract and other big cases. It has a Court of Appeal which hears appeals from the above three Courts and from County Courts, and a Court of Criminal Appeal, usually presided over by Judges of the Queen's Bench Division, which reviews sentences and convictions that are held to be questionable. The official name for the High Court is the Supreme Court of Judicature.

Who are exempt from jury service?

Foreigners who live in Britain, deaf and dumb people, nuns and anyone not on the electoral roll are disqualified from serving. Exempt also are peers, Members of Parliament, clergymen, barristers and solicitors and certain other officers of the Court, doctors, chemists, members of the armed forces, aircraft pilots, postmen, customs and inland revenue officers, policemen and officials of the royal household. A number of other people who have specialised jobs are also exempt. Exemption must be claimed or the person may be liable to serve on a jury.

How often may one be called for jury service?

Nobody is called more than once a year, and in practice one serves very rarely indeed, or not at all – at most, perhaps, on three occasions in a lifetime.

Must a person attend if summoned?

Yes; a summons has the weight of the law behind it and there are penalties for non-attendance, unless the summons was served late. A person may be excused jury duty by applying to the Sheriff and stating his reasons, which must be sound ones.

Are jurors paid?

Yes; they are paid travelling and subsistence allowances, and are also paid compensation for loss of earning while they are away from their usual work.

CHAPTER ELEVEN

SOLICITORS
AND
BARRISTERS

It has been said that a lawyer makes his living out of other people's ignorance. This, in part, is true. But the fact does not make his calling any less honourable, for when one reflects on it one realises that many professional people do precisely the same. An architect makes his living out of the inability of the builder to design a school or hospital, a doctor makes his money because his patients don't know what is wrong with them, a photographer because his clients cannot take the pictures themselves.

And whilst the law is often described as 'informed common sense' it needs a great deal more than common knowledge to interpret it.

Everyone, in law, is assumed to know the law, but it takes a solicitor five years of hard training even to get on nodding acquaintance with the multitudinous points that concern just one of the many divisions of the law.

Yes, we must admit that we need lawyers. Solicitors and barristers are there to see that we receive our just dues, whether they be compensation for an accident, full legal title to property – or six months in the lock-up. They have worked long years for their highly specialised knowledge, and today, a private citizen who thinks he can put his own case, if it is any but the simplest type, is either a genius or a misguided optimist.

Most people are a little confused about the different roles of solicitor and barrister. They are not sure of the different types of work they do, of which one they should approach for this or that reason. Following are some of the essential differences in the life and work of both branches of the profession.

Solicitors

A solicitor might be called the general practitioner of his profession. He may specialise in conveyancing, or divorce, or some other branch of the law, but he is also able to give general advice to his clients on a wide variety of legal problems when they come to his office. His job, one could say, is to lift the burden of legal work from the shoulders of the public, and either attend to it himself, or pass it on to a barrister if the nature of the work demands that he should.

The young man who wishes to enter this august profession should have had

A busy morning in the solicitor's office

a good general education at least up to the standard of the General Certificate of Education, 'A' level in two subjects and, to quote the *Law Society's Gazette*, possess absolute personal integrity, energy and drive, initiative, mental flexibility, and have an aptitude for the law.

The method of entering the profession is by serving articles. This means that he is 'apprenticed' to a solicitor – or firm of solicitors – for a period of usually five years (or a good deal less for a university law graduate), during which time he tries to accumulate knowledge in the various branches of the law. In the past his parents would have had to pay a premium for this training, but today he may actually receive a small salary for his doubtful assistance to his master. Whilst serving his articles he must also attend a law school for one year full time. After about two years he takes an intermediate examination, and at the completion of his articles a final examination. If he is successful he is then put on the Solicitors' Roll.

If the young solicitor has a private income he may then set up on his own in an office and wait for clients, but the usual procedure is to spend a few years learning practical law as a qualified assistant to an established solicitor and then look for a junior partnership.

The essence of a solicitor's job is diversity. The public who timidly knock on his office door have problems of many kinds, from selling a house to divorcing a spouse. He must listen to them all – with sympathy, with tact, and with understanding. He must be ready to give constructive advice on a thousand subjects, whether it be advice that will take his client into court, or advice to see a colleague who may have a greater knowledge of the particular subject.

A solicitor must be a kind of father confessor to his clients, and often to his clients' families; he must have a sound knowledge of commerce and the stock market, and he must have a deep understanding of the practice of the law. He must know how to keep silent when given a confidence by a client; he must be able to talk to the Court when the occasion demands. And, of course, he must be able to run an office and staff, and to keep accounts of both his own money and his clients.

A solicitor must, in fact, be all that most of us strive to be, but rarely succeed!

Barristers

Although a solicitor would probably disapprove of such a comparison, one could say that, if solicitors are the fine craftsmen of the profession, the barristers are the artists.

Their day-to-day life is very different from that of the solicitor, who deals directly with the public. A private citizen may knock on a solicitor's office door, be admitted and dealt with. A barrister cannot deal with the public directly; his clients must be solicitors. When a solicitor accepts a case from a person, and decides that it needs a barrister to represent the client in Court, he then passes the documents, called a brief, over to the chambers of the barrister of his choice, where the barrister's clerk accepts it. On the brief will be marked the fee that is offered to the barrister for his services.

Even the barrister's chambers are different from the busy office of a solicitor. Having no contact with the public, his studies are far less disturbed by the hurly-

A barrister pleads his case

burly of daily life. He sits in his study surrounded by his venerable books – and modern ones – and builds up his case in peace and quiet. He has no contact even with the business side of his own profession. His clerk will accept his brief and deal with any monetary problems that may arise.

The barrister's clerk is a most important individual. When a barrister starts in practice he rarely can afford to set up in separate chambers and have a clerk of his own, so he usually rents a room from one of his more established colleagues (who may have leased a suite of chambers in one of the Inns of Court), and shares a clerk with him and others who may be in the group. The newcomer does not enter into a partnership with his colleagues, but is completely independent except for the clerk he shares with them.

The barristers' clerk makes his living from 'commission' on the briefs that he accepts for his employers, and the salary that each pays him.

His importance lies in the fact that, whilst barristers themselves can indulge in no form of advertising, their clerk, who is in close contact with several solicitors, may act as his 'front man', advising his associates on the prowess of his employer in this or that type of case.

He has to employ tact and wisdom in his delicate job. If he thinks from past experience that the only barrister in his chambers who would be free when a certain case is brought before the Court would not be the right man for the case, he must, to safeguard his reputation, turn down the brief.

However, the commission that he earns encourages a clerk to bring in as many briefs to his chambers as can be handled by his barristers, and a good clerk can make his chambers' revenue very lucrative indeed.

The barrister's profession is an odd one in many ways. He must wait for his work, he must appear aloof from monetary matters, and he may not approach the public. But a busy junior barrister may make a very good living indeed, a living that would make many a senior executive in another profession green with envy. His knowledge and his manner may command fees of a very high figure if he has had continued success in court.

In every junior barrister's life there comes a day when he must decide to continue to be a successful junior or to 'take silk'. This is the granting of a patent as Queen's Counsel, and the move changes the type of work – and often reduces the income – of a successful junior. But as a Q.C. he is uncluttered by the behind-the-scenes work of the junior – although this is often well paid work – and can concentrate on taking the leading part in a case: that of an advocate. This decision requires some courage. It may cut a man off from some of his income, but it opens the door to the higher offices of British Justice.

CHAPTER TWELVE

SOME LEGAL TERMS

Abatement. Abatement (or reduction) of nuisance is the right of a person to lessen or remove any form of nuisance which prevents his quiet enjoyment of his garden, house, etc.

Abstract of Title. A summary of the title deeds, or chain of ownership, down to the current owner. An abstract of title is usually produced by the seller to help the buyer's solicitor investigate (check) the title.

Act of God. An insurance policy will often state that in the event of an Act of God the company is not liable to make good any loss incurred. Acts of God are those which happen without any assistance from man – flood, storm, earthquake, etc.

Ademption. If a person leaves an object in his will, then sells it or gives it away before he dies, the part of the will dealing with the object is automatically revoked. This is called ademption – the revocation of part of the will.

Affidavit. A written statement made on oath, which is, if the Court thinks fit, used in evidence.

Affiliation Order. A woman who is about to give birth to an illegitimate child, or has

done so within twelve months, may apply
to the Court for an affiliation order against
its father. If the man is proved to be the
father, then he may be ordered to pay up
to 50s a week to the mother for the
maintenance of the child. In many cases
he will have to continue to pay until the
child is 16 years old, or even longer. The
marriage of the mother to another man
does not necessarily revoke the order, as
a man is not expected to support the
illegitimate child of his wife.

Affirmation. Some people object to making
an oath in the normal way. They are
allowed to use the form of affirmation:
'I John Smith do solemnly, and sincerely,
and truly declare and *affirm* . . .' There are
penalties for those who perjure themselves under this affirmation, just as there
are for those who flout the oath.

Agent. A person who has the authority to
make agreements, sign contracts, etc., for
another.

Alien. Any person who, in Britain, is not
a British subject – a foreigner.

Appeal. If the decision of a Court is considered to be unjust an appeal may often
be made to a higher authority so that it

'It's all Greek to me!'
A layman puzzles over a complicated
legal document

can review the case and either alter the decision or order a new trial.

Arson. The wilful setting on fire of the property of another person, or setting fire to one's own property in an attempt to defraud an insurance company.

Articles of Association. The terms written in official form, under which a company will carry on the administration of its business. They regulate such matters as shareholders, directors, meetings of the company, etc.

Assault. Often confused with battery, assault is a threatening action to another person which is severe enough to instil fear of physical violence, or an actual attempt to commit an injury. Battery is the application of the force itself. Every battery must be preceded by an assault, hence the term 'assault and battery'.

Assizes. Courts of Law held regularly on circuit in England by H. M. judges for the administration of civil and criminal justice. In the Assizes the facts and the verdict may be decided by a jury.

Attorney at Law. A duly qualified practitioner and officer of the courts. Today he is called a solicitor.

Bail. Money or security for money deposited

at the court on behalf of a prisoner which allows him his freedom until his trial. If he fails to appear at court at the time when he must answer the charges against him, bail is forfeit. Always think carefully before providing bail for a prisoner.

Bankrupt. A person whose debts are more than his assets and whom a Court has ordered to surrender his goods to pay his creditors, is known as a bankrupt.

Barrister. Solicitors deal directly with everyday clients, but barristers usually can only accept their work from solicitors. The brief (the facts of the case and a summary of the evidence that his witnesses will give) is supplied to him by a solicitor. After studying a brief, the barrister – a member of the legal profession who has passed certain examinations which entitle him to the right to appear in the various superior courts – then presents the case to the judge (and jury).

By-Law. Parliament cannot make laws to cover every small local condition and so delegates some of its authority to local councils, who pass by-laws. They may deal with grazing rights, building construction, roads, local services and so on. They have the full power of the law behind them.

Canon Law. The laws laid down in the Canons of the Established Church.

Capital Crimes. All crimes punishable by death are called capital crimes. Today they are:

(*a*) Any murder done in the course of furtherance of theft.

(*b*) Any murder by shooting or causing an explosion.

(*c*) Any murder done in the course of or for the purpose of resisting arrest, or in order to effect or assist an escape from legal custody.

(*d*) Any murder of a police officer acting in the execution of his duty or of any person assisting him in that duty.

(*e*) In the case of a person who is a prisoner at the time, any murder of a prison officer acting in the execution of his duty or of any person assisting him in that duty.

Other capital crimes are treason, piracy with violence, and setting fire to a ship of war.

Caveat Emptor (Let the buyer beware). The legal phrase used in purchases where the seller does not assume responsibility for the condition of the goods sold.

Chancery. The division of the High Court of Justice, dealing with cases relating to land, wills, trusts, etc.

Chattels. All movable property used for domestic and other purposes are called personal chattels, and interests in leasehold land are termed real chattels.

Collusion. An agreement between husband and wife to deceive the Court in order to be divorced is collusion, and as such would prevent the divorce if it were discovered.

Common Law. The law that has been built up over the centuries by custom and precedent. Common law will not be found in the Statute Book, never having been passed as Acts of Parliament, but it is recognised law, and breaking it has the usual consequences.

Compounding an Offence. If a person knows that a crime has been committed and takes a reward from someone for not disclosing it, he is said to have compounded an offence.

Condonation. A term used in divorce cases when the offended party has forgiven the offence and allowed it to make no difference in the relationship between them in marriage. A divorce action which later uses the offence as its basis would not be successful.

Connivance. Another divorce case term. When a husband or wife knows of a marital offence committed by one or the other at the time, and either consents to it or does nothing about it, connivance is present.

Contempt of Court. Misbehaviour connected with Court proceedings likely to obstruct justice, or the disobeying of a Court instruction. A judge can imprison the person until he considers the contempt has been purged.

Copyright. The exclusive right of an author of any work to control its publication. Merely by writing a letter, the writer creates a copyright on it unless he has made other arrangements. No other formality is necessary. Copyright generally lasts throughout the author's lifetime and for a term of fifty years after his death.

Crown. The Sovereign, or the State acting for the Sovereign.

Damages. Money awarded by the Court as compensation for loss or injuries received.

Deed. A formal document which sets out the terms agreed between the parties. A deed must be *signed, sealed and delivered.* Consideration for obligations is presumed.

Defamation. If a person's name is injured by a statement, spoken or in writing, then he may go to law and attempt to recover damages for the damage to his reputation brought about by the defamation.

Dilapidations. Defects in a dwelling that a tenant must make good during or at the end of his tenancy.

Domicile. The permanent country of residence of a person which he intends to keep indefinitely – his legal home. Although living for several years in the South of France, a person may be domiciled in London, where his main home is or was situated and where he intends to return.

Duress. Threats of force that would make a person do something that he did not wish to do.

Earnest. Something which is given as a pledge, or for sealing a bargain.

Easement. The right of using another's land for a particular purpose. The right of way over a piece of private land is an easement.

Embezzlement. The use, or stealing, of money by a person, after it has been put into his hands for another purpose.

Entail. To bestow land or property on a person and his heirs, without allowing them the right to dispose of the property.

Equity. Occasionally the law was found to be too harsh. Equity is a system of rules which has grown up over the centuries and is applied by the Courts to ensure that what is 'morally right and fair' should be done.

Escrow. The deed of transfer to a house of which the sale has not yet been completed is an escrow. In other words, a document held, perhaps by a solicitor, until the full conditions on which the document is to come into force have been carried out.

Ex Gratia. An ex gratia payment may be made by an employer to his workman if an accident has occurred at work that is not the employer's fault. The payment is made out of sympathy for his employee, not from legal necessity.

Fee Simple. The opposite of entailed property. Estate in fee simple can be disposed of in any way the owner pleases.

Foreclosure. The action that may be taken by the lender of money on mortgage by which be bars the right of the mortgagor to redeem the mortgage property. The security (house, etc.) becomes the mortgagee's property if the foreclosure action succeeds.

Felony. An offence or crime that is more serious than a misdemeanor. Murder, robbery, arson, treason, are felonies. The line between the two is sometimes a little hazy.

Habeas Corpus. A procedure by which a person may, on behalf of another who has been arrested, question before a judge the legality of the arrest and imprisonment.

Hearsay. Evidence that is second hand. If a witness states that he heard a person report what another person said then the evidence is hearsay, and not admissible in court.

Homicide. The killing of one human being by another. This falls into three main categories: *Justifiable homicide,* which includes a legal execution, self-defence, killing during the putting down of riots if there is no other way of quelling them, and killing to prevent a violent crime against another person. *Excusable homicide* is accidental killing, or on certain occasions killing in self-defence. *Felonious homicide* is deliberate and unlawful killing of another person.

Until recently killing or attempting to kill oneself (suicide) was a crime, but the law has been changed and it is not now punishable. To be classed as homicide, death from the injury must take place no longer than a year and a day after it is inflicted.

In Camera. A case from which the public is excluded is held in camera. The word camera means a room, and implies secrecy.

Indemnity. The making good of loss or damage to the person indemnified. An insurance company indemnifies a person against accident in a motor car, or on holiday, etc.

Indictment. Before a trial takes place the prisoner must be indicted. The indictment is usually a written official document accusing him of the offence, which must be specified in the document.

Injunction. A Court order stopping someone from doing damage to another person, his property, or preventing his quiet enjoyment of it. An injunction to restrain can be made for many reasons, from turning the volume down on a radio to keeping a dog in order.

Intestacy. When a person dies without making any form of will he dies intestate; the situation is called intestacy.

Larceny. The taking away of another's property for one's own use; theft. Petty larceny is the stealing of goods of small value.

Law Reports. For several hundred years law cases have been written down and then published. If a lawyer can find no actual statute on a legal point in question, he can refer to these reports and use the findings in them as a precedent and guide to his present case. If an exactly similar question was judged in a certain way even centuries ago the judgment is still good law today, providing it has not been overruled in a later case, or by an Act passed since the case was heard.

Legacy. An item of property or money left to a person in a will.

Legal Aid. If a person cannot afford to pay for representation in court he can apply for legal aid from the Secretary of his Legal Aid Area. Legal aid may be for the services of a solicitor or, where necessary, a barrister. General inquiries may be made at The Law Society, Bell Yard, Strand, London W.C.2.

Legislation. The making of laws by Parliament.

Libel. Any published written or printed statement that may cause a person to be lowered in the estimation of right-thinking members of society. Libel can also take the form of a cartoon, painting, etc.

Lien. The right to hold another's goods or property until he fulfils his duty regarding it – such as completing a payment. A garage proprietor can, in certain circumstances, hold a customer's car until he has been paid for his work.

Liquidator – *see* Receiver.

Magna Carta. Originally the Great Charter signed by King John in 1215, and now used to include any major constitutional document relating to the rights of the common man.

Majority. A person attains his or her majority the day before his 21st birthday.

Malicious Prosecution. Unjustifiably accusing a person of a crime, and prosecuting with the object of casting a doubt on his good character.

Manslaughter. Unlawfully killing a human being without malice. It may be deliberate or involuntary, but it must be without premeditation. However, if someone is caught stealing and accidentally shoots the person who attempts to stop him he may be charged with murder, just as a person who intends only to injure another may be charged with murder if the person dies from his wounds.

Market Overt. Open market. If a person buys goods, say on a stall at a country market where the goods are openly displayed, and later they are found to be stolen, he will not have to give them back to the original owner. If the sale had been private he would have had to give them back.

Messuage. A house (flat, etc.) and its various outbuildings.

Misdemeanour. Illegal behaviour. Broadly speaking a name for those offences that are considered less serious than felonies, although the borderline is sometimes very indistinct. All offences were at one time divided into three categories: treason, an offence against the Crown or State; felony, serious crimes that were punishable by death; and misdemeanours, the lesser crimes.

Muniments. The deeds, papers, documents, etc., relating to the ownership of land.

Notary. A public officer who is qualified to administer oaths, supervise the signing of contracts, deeds, and generally authenticate them by *noting* particularly where the documents are to be sent abroad.

Nuisance. Private nuisance is the act of causing a person to lose some of the amenities to which he is entitled – i.e. enjoyment of his garden. Public nuisance deprives the public of their rightful amenities.

Nullity of Marriage. A decree of nullity may be made when there has been no real marriage, due to the youth of one of the parties, a previous marriage, close kinship, or lack of consent on the part of the bride or groom, non-consummation, or a number of other reasons. Nullity, unlike divorce, is not the breaking of a marriage: it is the statement that the marriage did not legally exist.

Quarter Sessions. A Court of a Borough or County that tries cases in which a jury is necessary. It also hears appeals from a Magistrates' Court.

Patent. A monopoly granted to the first inventor of a machine, appliance, etc. Letters Patent ensure that his invention will not be made and marketed by anyone else for a limited time. The address of the

Patent Office is Southampton Buildings, Chancery Lane, London W.C.2.

Perjury. The offence of giving false evidence under oath in court.

Per Pro Signature. A signature made by an agent – a person who has been empowered to sign for another. Usually abbreviated to p.p.

Petty Sessions. Magistrates' Courts attended by one or more magistrates for dealing with small offences, or for remitting a person for trial by a higher Court.

Plaintiff. The person who brings a suit to court and *complains* against a defendant.

Probation. A sentence may be suspended and an offender put under the care of a probation officer. He is free to carry out his normal domestic life, but he must report to the probation officer regularly and notify any change of address or employment. The officer in turn acts as adviser. A person of any age may be put on probation, but this is usually reserved for young first offenders.

Receiver, or Liquidator. Officials or other persons who receive and administer the rents, incomes, etc., from businesses that are being wound up under court order, or

297

persons who have been declared bankrupt.

Recorder. The magistrate or judge presiding over Quarter Sessions.

Reversion. When a lease expires, property *reverts* to the landlord. This is the right of reversion of the owner of the ground or building.

Revoke. To cancel, withdraw, make void.

Search Warrant. A document signed by a magistrate empowering the Police to enter and search premises.

Slander. A false and malicious statement spoken by a person which injures the reputation of another. Slander may give rise to a civil action.

Stale Cheque. A cheque paid to a person and presented by him to his bank more than six months later is regarded as a stale cheque and usually will not be valid unless special arrangements are made.

Statute. A law made by an Act of Parliament.

Subpoena. A summons demanding a person's attendance at court. There are penalties for ignoring a subpoena. The term means 'under penalty'.

Summary Offences. Small offences that are heard before justices of the peace and are dealt with rapidly – such as motoring offences, etc.

Tenement. A house (flat, etc.) occupied by a tenant.

Title. The right of ownership of property, houses, lands.

Tort. A wrong (civil, as opposed to criminal) done by one person to another or to his property. If a man fails to control his dangerous animal so that it escapes and attacks another he has committed a tort. The principal torts are nuisance, negligence and defamation of character.

Void. Vacant, empty, that which has no legal force.

Ward of Court. A young person, under the age of 21, who is under the guardianship of a person appointed by the Court or of the Court itself. Interference with the rights of a ward may be treated as a contempt.

Writ. Most usually it is the document by which a plaintiff starts a court action in a civil case – a document of the Crown which requires a person to obey its demands. A writ is issued to a defendant summoning him to a court.

INDEX

A

Accidents

    By cyclists, 24–25
    In neighbour's house, 23–24
    In public, 22, 25–26
    Pedestrian accidents, 25–26
Adoption of children, 84
Adoption, qualifications necessary, 86
Animal strays, 30
Animals in gardens, 27
Assizes, 260

B

Bailiffs, 122
Bankruptcy, definition of, 120–121
Bankruptcy, discharge from, 121–122
Bankruptcy, wife's possessions, 121
Bigamy, 47–48
Birth certificate, 70–71
Birth, registering of, 72
Breach of promise, 48–49
British Railways, compensation for injury,
    35–36
British Railways, responsibility for time-
    tables, 36

C

Car purchase

   Late delivery by dealer, 175
   Ownership during H.P., 159–160
   Repossessing by finance company, 161
   Written guarantees, 159

Care and protection, children in need of, 87–88

Central Criminal Court, 262

Children

   Buying of cigarettes, 82
   Employment of, 81–82
   Illegitimate, 69–72
   Non-attendance at school, 89
   Religious education of, 89
   Stage work, 82
   Working hours under fifteen, 256

Commercial vehicle driving, permitted hours, 177

Compulsory purchase of property, 208–209

County Courts, 262

Courts of Law, Juvenile, 260

Courts of Summary Jurisdiction, 259–260

Cycle lights, 180

Cyclists

   Carrying extra passengers, 180

Cyclists *(continued)*
    Dangerous riding, 179
    Parking, 178
    Racing on roads, 178
    Under the influence of drink, 178

D

Debts, imprisonment for, 122–123
Debts, responsibility of husband, 49, 50, 52
Debts, responsibility of unmarried couples,
    54
Divorce
    Absolute, 60–61
    Adultery, 55–56
    Co-Respondent, 63
    Cost of divorce, 63
    Cruelty, 56–57
    Defended suit, 60
    Desertion, 56
    Division of property, 65
    Divorce nisi, 60–61
    Failure of petition, 57–58
    Foreign decrees, 57
    Guardianship of children, 66
    Grounds for divorce, 55
    Payment to wife by husband, 64
    Starting divorce proceedings, 59
Dogs, responsibility for, 27–28

E

Employees and rival firms, 249
Employees' damage to work equipment, 249
Employees, duties to employers, 245
Employees' inventions, ownership of, 250
Employees, payment of wages while sick, 251
Employers, duties to employees, 245
Employers, payment of wages in goods, 251
Employers, responsibilities for damage caused by employees, 249
Employment, notice in absence of written contract, 246, 248
Employment, reasons for immediate dismissal, 246
Employment, testimonials, 248, 251
Evidence at court, wife's obligations, 54

F

Factories Act, 1961, 252
Family Allowance, ownership of, 53
Fences, 19
Fences, party property, 19
Fires in gardens, 19–20
Foster parents, definition of, 88

G

Guardian, definition of, 87

H

High Courts, work of, 263

Hire purchase

Agreement forms, 124–125
Contracts made by wife, 52
Damage to goods, 115
Final payment, 115
Recovery of goods, 114
Redress for defective goods, 107, 159
Repossession of car if payments delayed, 161

Home confinement grant, 73

Hotels

Booking claims, 32
Loss of goods, 31
Payment of bill, 31–32
Responsibility of travel agent, 32–33

House, joint ownership, 53

Housekeeping savings, ownership of, 50

House purchase

Definition of freehold, 189

House purchase *(continued)*

    Definition of leasehold, 189–190

    Definition of mortgage, 193

    Form of contract, 189

    General costs of, 203–205

    How to obtain a mortgage, 193

    Liability of hidden defects, 205–206

    Mortgagee's right to enter, 200–201

    Mortgagee's right to repossess, 199–200

    Mortgages and life assurance, 195–196

    Mortgages and married women, 196–7

    Normal deposit, 192

    Number of mortgaged properties that may be owned, 200

    Remortgages, 197

    Second mortgages, 198

    Selling before repayment of mortgage, 197

    Solicitors' charges, 203–205

    'Subject to contract', 190–192

    Types of mortgage, 195–196

I

Infants

    Definition of an infant, 73–76

    Hire purchase by, 77

    Injuries to, 76

Infants *(continued)*

    Ownership of property, 76

    Responsibility for crimes, 78–80

    Torts and civil wrongs, 78

Intestacy, 102–103

I.O.U.s, 115

J

Jury service, 262, 264–265

L

Land registration, 202

Leasehold, expiry, 201

Leasehold, typical agreement for purchase of a flat, 211–220

Legal terms, 281–299

Letters of administration, 102

Libel, 11

Licence, dog, 26

Limitations Act, 21

Limited companies

    Cost of forming, 119

    Forming of, 118

    Private and public, 117–118

    Purpose of forming by small business man, 116–117

M

Maintenance action by wife for non-payment, 61–62

Maintenance orders, 61–62, 64, 65

Marriage

Arrangements for church ceremony, 42

At Registry Office, 42–43

Change of name by, 50–51

Kinship restrictions, 44–46

Legal responsibilities, 49–50

Marriage certificate, 40–41

Necessary consent, 39

Of divorced persons, 65

Requirements, 39

Special licence, 44

Times of day permitted, 42

To foreign subjects, 47

Void marriages, 46–48

Maternity allowance, 73

Maternity grant, 72–75

Motor sport accidents, 22

Motoring

Accidentally killing animals, 155

Attendance in Court, when obligatory, 170–171

Motoring *(continued)*
    Authority of Highway Code, 162
    Careless driving, 166–167
    Categories of offences, 169–170
    Charges for speeding, 172
    Concealed turning signs, 177
    Contacting police after accident, 155–156
    Damage to car by dog, 155
    Dangerous driving, 164–165
    Disqualification and 'special reasons', 166
    Driving licence, 151, 174–175
    Drunk in charge, 167–168
    Effect of private 'No Parking' sign, 162
    Endorsement on licence, 168
    Fitting of sirens or bells, 171
    Fitting of windows in vans, 174
    Five-year test, 173
    Five-year test details, 182–185
    Insurance, 151–152
    Motoring organisations, help from, when charged, 172
    Motoring under influence of drink or drugs, 167
    Necessary basic condition of vehicle, 181–185
    Obstruction, definition of, 164
    On motorways, 173
    Owners' responsibilities, 153–156, 175–7

Motoring *(continued)*
    Parking off the road, 156
    Parking without lights, 171
    Police action after accident, 155–156, 181–182
    Qualifications necessary, 173
    Racing on public roads, 169
    Reasons for disqualification, 169–170
    Responsibility for learner driver, 152-3
    Road Fund Licence, 152
    School Crossing Patrols, 177
    Speed limits for goods vehicles, 156
    Sports car passengers' cover, 158
    Stationary car in gear, 169
    Sub-standard repairs, 162
    Use of commercial vehicle for private purposes, 174
    Warning of prosecution after offence, 170
    Wife's insurance cover, 158
    Zebra crossings, 175–177

N

Name, change of, 34
Negligence, 13
Noise at night, 14
Noise, general, 14–15
Nuisance, 13–16, 19–21

P

Parents, legal duties of, 86
Pets, ownership of, 26–30
Picketing during strikes, 256
Probation, 80
Property, wife's ownership of, 53

Purchase

Defects in used car, 159
Delivery dates of goods, 110–111
Seller's description of goods, 108–109, 113
Shopkeepers' prices, 111–112
Stolen goods, 107–108
Sub-standard food, 111
Weight of goods, 113
Purchase tax on vehicles, 173–174

Q

Quarter Sessions, 263

R

Radios, noisy, 13–14
Rates

Definitions of, 206

Rates *(continued)*
    Increase of, for rent-controlled property, 227–8
    Method of assessment (1963), 206
    Objection to valuation, and appeal, 207–208
Receipts, stamps on, 116
Rent-controlled property
    Death of tenant, 226–227
    Sale of by landlord, 226
    Security of tenure, 223
    Serving of notice, 223–224
Rent controls, 223, 227-228, 229
Rented accommodation
    Advisability of written agreement, 230
    Assignment of lease, 232–233
    'Fair wear and tear', 233
    Fire, 233–234
    Fixtures and fittings, 234, 235
    Furnished accommodation, 229
    Furnished flat, definition of, 229–230
    Notice, 223–224
    Payments falling in arrears, 231–232
    Rent-controlled flats, 223
    Repairs by landlord, 228
    Responsibilities of tenants, 233, 234
    Sub-letting, 228–232
    Typical tenancy agreement, 236–242

Rented property, alternative accommodation, 225–226
Restaurants, food quality, 30–31
Restaurants, payment for meals, 30
Right of light, 16–18
Road Fund Licence, display of, 152
Roots on neighbouring land, 18

S

Separation, legal, 61
Shops, early closing, 252–254
Slander, 11–12
Solicitors and Barristers, 270–278
Solicitors' fees, 34–35
Stealing by finding, 33–34
Sunday working, 254

T

Title, abstract of, 203
Title of property, 201–202
Tort, death of defendant, 33
Tort, responsibility of husband for wife, 49
Torts, 12–13
Trespass, by animals, 27, 28
Trespassing, 21
Trespassing, responsibility for, 52

W

Wills

After marriage, 53
Codicils, 95
Copies of, 98
Creditors' interest in, 102
Definition of, 93
Executors, 54, 97–98
Family Provisions Inheritance Act, 100–101
Forms of, 93–94
Making of, 98
Minimum age for making, 95–96
Proving of the will, 99–100, 102
Purpose of, 93
Revoked wills, 96–97
Rights of unborn children, 77
Signatures, 94
Solicitors' charges for making, 98–99
Specimen, 103–104
Unfair will, 100–101
Use of legal terms, 95

Z

Zebra crossings, rights of walkers on, 175–177